Be Yourself to Free Yourself

AWAKENING TO THE LIFE
YOU ARE MEANT TO LIVE

Monica Moody

© 2021 by Monica Moody

ISBN: 978-1-7366133-0-6 (paperback) | ISBN: 978-1-7366133-1-3 (ebook)

Library of Congress Control Number: 2021903648

Book Cover Design by Nathaniel Dasco

Interior Design by Ljiljana Pavkov

Printed in Stockbridge, Georgia

For more information, visit www.owningchange.com.

Alternative Permission:
Please reprint and share any part of this book with anyone who might benefit from it. The only request is that you please include the following with any portion you share or reprint:

Reprinted with permission from the author, Monica Moody (www.owningchange.com).

OwningChange

*To every person who would dare to trust
the love and guidance of their own soul.*

*And to my dude and partner, Willis.
Everyone should be blessed with a "you."*

Be
Yourself
to Free
Yourself

Table of Contents

Acknowledgements

Love and gratitude to the teachers who inspired my path and elevated my life: Wayne Dyer, Marianne Williamson, Eckhart Tolle, Gary Zukav, Reverend Deborah L. Johnson, Jerry & Esther Hicks and "Abraham," Kahlil Gibran, and Jalāl ad-Dīn Muhammad Rūmī, also known as Rumi. Your hearts and wisdom are woven into the pages of this book.

To my fabulous book publishing and launch coach, Diana M. Needham. What a blessing you have been throughout this entire process. Thank you for being the exact, sweet, guiding, and loving presence that I needed.

Appreciation to my editor, Iuliana Marin, who is a language and grammar master. Thank you for making the editing process seamless.

To my tribe! My siblings who sit in the middle of my heart, Kenny, Edward, Jina, Linda, Junior, Michelle, Pam, Gary, Reggie and Stanley. And to my dad, Huely and my mom, Aristene, who beautifully raised us all. Each one of you and your partners and offspring feed me daily. I am blessed to call you fam.

To my in-laws, with Helen leading the way. You have loved me in ways that constantly remind me of God's goodness. And to you Garnetta, for always being there as a safe space to land when I need a good laugh and an emotional hideaway.

My girls, Taylor, and Sydni. I am moved by your beauty and light. Your brilliance inspires me, your humor and wit enliven me, and your personhood keeps me grounded, every single day. I am in awe of the fact that God would gift me with the privilege of being your mom.

To my bonus daughter, Whitney. Yes, girl. Your love and light changed me and made me a better person in every way. I feel so very blessed by your presence in my life. Thank you for the joy that you bring.

My husband, Willis, you have made my life easy and wonderful, and I thank you for being all that you are. Thank you for supporting my work and thank you for supporting me. This book is the summary of a path that you enabled in many ways, as we have grown together. You make me feel blessed and loved every day.

For the unconditional love of my DFF, Ulisa, life-long bestie, Tanu, "church" partner, Mary-Elizabeth, joyful sister, Sherall, Soul Sister, Clara, travel buddy, Josette, and my "Dumb Family", Arthur, Mimi, Linda, Kassy, Stacey and Schonette. To all of my buddies. Your friendship is everything.

And to all of the brave souls who commit to becoming the better world that we hope for. Your resolve to be the love and the light that we all crave will forever inspire me.

Now that you have your copy of *Be Yourself to Free Yourself: Awakening to the Life You Are Meant to Live*, you are on your way towards learning how to powerfully align with your soul and reclaim your authentic power! Plus, you will soon be equipped with tools and strategies that will aid you in moving towards your goals and dreams, with greater ease and grace.

As a thank you for purchasing my book, you'll also receive access to several special bonuses I created to support you on your journey, including, (1) the **True You Personal Branding Playbook**, to assist you with bringing your personal and professional presence in alignment with the True You, (2) the **True You Meditation**, for sustained inspiration and renewal and (3) the **Be Yourself to Free Yourself Facilitator's Guide** for book clubs, so you can experience the book in community, for even greater accountability and impact, should you desire.

You can claim all of the bonus gifts here:
https://www.owningchange.com/true-you-bonus-gifts.
And as another bonus, you'll receive periodic tips, tools and inspiration as a part of the Owning Change Community.

The sooner you learn how to truly allow your soul to take the lead, the sooner you get to live the liberated life you are meant to live. I'm in your corner and absolutely cheering you on.

Let me know if I can assist you in any way. Here's to powerfully living as the True You!

"It doesn't work if we're not allowed to be who we are.
Behavior modification is a soul silencer.
It is a mute button on our souls."
– MELANIE DEWBERRY

Introduction

It was never supposed to be so hard. And with all of nature, except for humans, it isn't. Whether we're observing a horse grazing peacefully in a pasture or a tree standing majestically by a stream, we get the sense that these living organisms are fully and completely at one with all that is.

There's no struggle. No grappling. No warring against their own nature. And as we take in their presence, there's a part of us that stands in recognition of what it feels like to be so powerfully aligned with who and what we really are.

The strong sense of "okayness" that we experience from simply observing nature is the evidence. We do remember. But how is it that we ever forgot?

As a woman who has finally come to own her worthiness, I can say that it feels as if my soul has been in constant pursuit of me my entire life, working to remind me of who I am. I have images of the folks who wait for travelers at the airport with signs bearing their names.

As I look back, I see my soul everywhere, holding one of those signs, "Monica Moody. This way!" Each sign, the equivalent of a silent call saying, "Wake up, my dear! Remember."

And with a voice that now feels faint, feeble, and weak by comparison, the world beyond my soul called me too, confusing me and attempting to keep me small, disconnected, and afraid.

This voice was born from painful experiences, from an ego that wanted to protect me and from jarring messages and conditioning from the outside world. Together, they took a powerhouse of a little world-changing girl and convinced her to fear just about everything, including her power.

But one day, in a beautiful moment of grace, she remembered. She directed her attention towards the voice of her soul. And this, my friend, changed everything.

The more I tuned in, the more I began to awaken to my true nature. And the more I opened to this aspect of myself, the more my life began to adjust to match the beauty that I was experiencing inside.

How I viewed myself changed. My relationships shifted. My career came into alignment. Abundance began to flow freely. Powerful synchronistic moments and miracles landed at my door. And life started to and continues to become sweeter and sweeter. All from making the choice to align with the truest aspect of my being, the True Me, my soul.

All of us, particularly in surrendered moments, have glimpses of our true nature. When we erupt in laughter. When we lose ourselves in the exquisiteness of something that we find beautiful. Or when we open our hearts to the felt presence of love.

These moments represent who we are in our most natural state, the state in which we are one with our souls, with God or the Universe itself. I call it a "state of grace." It's the space in which we are meant to dwell. It's home.

In "Everything You Need You Have," author Gerod Kite describes "home" as the "permanent place inside yourself where you are always okay." Indeed. And we get to live from this space. We don't have to stumble into it and settle for momentary peeks at our power. When we learn to tune into who we truly are and give that version of ourselves permission to take the lead, then we can launch the lives we are meant to live.

Why This Matters, Especially Now

Our world is in pain. Everywhere we look, we see struggle and heartache amid what appears to be a collection of failing systems that seem to be incapable of meeting our needs. From our woes with government and politics to widespread economic inequities and social injustice, there is much work to do.

And so, we show up on every front, armed for battle, trying to fix the things "out there." However, what we fail to realize is the fact that the world is in pain because far too many of us are in pain, which will continue to be the case as long as we are disconnected from our true, divine nature.

The world is a reflection of who we are. As within, so, without. This is the case in our individual lives, and it's also true for the collective. So, our efforts are misguided when we reach out into the world to try to fix a pain that's emanating from within. We may have temporary wins, but they are not sustainable, and they are mere patches on a bleeding world. Our charge is not to *fix* the world; we must *become* the better world we hope for. And we do this by returning to our true nature; returning to that blessed state of grace.

What a powerful invitation. Remember who you are, follow the guidance of your own soul, and focus solely on directing your inner world, and THEN, not only will you tap into a level of liberation that will beautify your own life, but you will also, by default, help to liberate and beautify this world.

The Purpose of This Book

Sometimes, when reading reviews on spiritual books, I'm amused when a reader says, "There's nothing new here. Same ideas, said differently." I find it humorous because I understand that the reviewer, though well-intentioned, I'm sure, is likely waiting for some silver bullet that will never come. Because, as noted in Ecclesiastes 1:9, "There is nothing new under the sun."

Universal truth is universal truth. It always has been and always will be. All any spiritual guide or teacher will ever be able to do is share their insights and point to these truths through the lens of their own life.

Your soul knows who you were born to be. And, if you are still expanding towards reaching your highest potential, as we all are, then the purpose of this book is to help you take your place. Regardless of where you are on your journey, if you have made your way here, chances are, we are simply kindred spirits who speak a common language, here to share in a sweet sacred space for this moment in time.

There are far too many beautiful souls circling in painful patterns, searching outside of themselves to find solutions to the troubles that ail them. There are too many souls walking through their days feeling frustrated and powerless to effect change in their lives and in the world, unaware of their inherent power and how to use it. And there are too many souls who are living beneath the levels of peace, joy, and happiness that could be theirs to enjoy.

A world of boundless grace and wonder is beckoning us to come closer. And it demands that we put down fear-based ways of living and pick up love. We can feel that the old ways don't fit anymore. But we're still scrambling in the dark, trying to find a light switch that can only be found inside ourselves. This book carves out a path for how to find, free, and grow that light.

The Path

From the moment I took my first conscious steps on my own spiritual journey, there was a part of me that knew that what I was learning was not just for me. I detailed the steps and documented my insights along the way. At times, I even found myself visualizing myself on stage and sharing my insights with others. Eventually, I became a Certified Life Purpose and Career Coach and a corporate trainer, and the lessons of my own life leapt into the lessons that I began to teach. These lessons and insights have been packaged into a model called the Owning Change Model of Transformation, which continues to serve both me and my clients, and I offer it to you freely and with boundless love.

There are four parts that represent the path towards liberation and a fully lived life: Awaken, Align, Flow & Love. Each part was birthed organically and represents the work done in the various phases of my own journey. I share the details of the stories that mark these defining moments, and I do so with as much vulnerability and openness as I can. I recognize that the very last thing you need is a photoshopped version of a carefully framed success story. You need and deserve an honest rendering of what it looks like to walk the path of conscious awakening, and I make every attempt to give you just that.

Part I, Awaken, is about examining your beliefs and remembering who you are. You will learn to quiet the noise around you so you can begin to tune to your own guidance. Align, Part II, is where you will learn about the laws of the Universe and how to use them to bring all aspects of your life into alignment with the desires of your soul.

Part III, Flow, is the pivotal point where you will learn the art and power of surrender and allowance. And finally, in Part IV, Love, we will take a detailed look at what it means to powerfully live as the most authentic version of you, what I call the "True You", in key areas of your life, from relationships, money, and career to parenting, social justice, and activism.

You will find that each phase of the model unlocks certain characteristics that, once embodied, power our path. These are "soul qualities," and they reflect your true nature and beauty. The word "nature" itself is derived from the Latin word "natura," which means "essential qualities" or "innate disposition," and these qualities represent the inherent qualities of your soul. Though the dimensions of our souls are boundless, the qualities that I detail are self-awareness, authenticity, vulnerability, responsibility, resilience, humility, and grace. Learning to embody these qualities will positively reshape every aspect of your life and amplify your power in the world.

The Language

When I first felt the pull towards doing the work that I do, I felt a level of intimidation around it. I was unsure of myself and what I knew. For years, I struggled with my angle and approach, and a big piece of that was figuring out what language was appropriate and right for me. I wanted to use a language and a framework that spoke to others, but it was vital that I use my own native tongue. I was not interested in translating my thoughts into words that felt safe, comfortable, and acceptable for others but flat and uninspiring for me.

As I share my ideas, you will see that I use several words interchangeably. For example, "that something greater," "Life," the "Universe," "Source," and "God" are synonymous to me, and they all point to what can best be described as infinite intelligence, ultimate consciousness, or the space from which we all emerged.

I also use words like "best self," "soul self," and "True You," which all describe what I believe to be the eternal, divine part of each and every being, that flows as an extension of God, or consciousness itself.

These and other phrases are a part of my own personal lexicon, which has resulted naturally and organically as I have grown and evolved over time. Staying true to a language that is comfortable and right for me ensures that you get unfiltered access to the purest version of my own soul's inspirations, and something tells me that you wouldn't have it any other way.

How to Approach This Book

As you consume the words in this book, challenge yourself to be led by your heart. We recognize those things that are true for us, based on how we feel. If there's an ounce of resonance in something that's shared, open to it and sit with it. Invite it to reveal all that you need to know. And if there are parts that do not feel true for you, then leave them where they are. The old saying, "eat the fish and spit out the bones", is sage advice.

Also, please know that as you move forward on your path of awakening, you will grow into deeper and deeper levels of truth. What rings true for you today, may shift tomorrow. New revelations will always come. Leave space for it all. For our purposes, as you dive into this book, please open your heart and allow yourself to be inspired by what moves you in this moment. May you receive all that you came for and more.

PART I:
AWAKEN

My Defining Moment of Grace

"I experienced, by the grace of God, a spiritual awakening, which was to lead me to a richer, fuller, more productive life."
– JOHN COLTRANE

My husband was in the yard working when I returned from running errands. As I headed for the door, he told me, with a kind and innocent enthusiasm, that he had rented some movies for us to watch. I'm not sure what had happened that caused my crabby mood, but with a shocking nastiness and dismissiveness, I said, "It doesn't matter what you rented. You never get anything I want to see anyway." As the words poured from my mouth, I looked up, and in a moment that stunned me, I clearly saw my burdened little self through my husband's eyes. His look pierced my soul.

I didn't know what had caused the heaviness I was feeling, and I didn't know what had prompted me to lash out, but what I did know, in the flash of that moment, was that I wanted to change. I no longer wanted to be the person who was at the mercy of the weights that she carried. I was ready to be free.

There's a Buddhist saying that "When the student is ready, the teacher will appear." My teacher, and the moment that initiated my awakening, was a literal fall down the stairs.

At the time, I was managing my first business, providing on-site spa services and events. I worked with a team of about 75 wellness professionals, including estheticians, massage therapists, and nail technicians, and we would go into homes and corporations and transform spaces into temporary, luxurious spas. Not only did we provide the equipment and supplies like massage tables, manicure stations, and spa products, but we also brought in a host of heavy fixtures, fountains, and decorative pieces to create a soothing and enchanting atmosphere. The work was extremely labor intensive, and it was steadily taking a toll on my back. I was in so much pain at one event that I decided to lie down inside of a closet at the client's house so no one would see me, praying for some relief.

What happened next was the proverbial insult that was added to my already painful injury. One day, as I was making my way down my stairs at home, the leg of my pants got stuck under my foot, and I slipped and fell from top to bottom, with each stair taking its personal jab at my back. The pain felt on par with childbirth, which was fitting perhaps because it did indeed give way to a birthing, but this time, it was my own. I landed in bed for months, waiting for an impending surgery.

Suddenly, I found myself in the middle of a stew of physical and emotional pain, mixed with a ton of mental baggage and deeply rooted insecurities. The perfect climate for a spiritual awakening.

At the peak of the pain, I had a huge argument with my husband and subsequently had my own internal meltdown. I was so worn and weary that I grabbed a bottle of drugs prescribed for my back, climbed out of bed, and somehow made my way to the car. I had a plan that did not involve a return, but thankfully, my husband intervened. I'm not sure that I would have followed through on that plan if he hadn't, but I was certainly headed to a hotel to sit in contemplation.

Enter grace.

Through a series of synchronistic events, resources (mostly in the form of books and people) begin to find their way to my door. The first was a book by Marianne Williamson called, "The Gift of Change," followed by her most popular book, "A Return to Love." Later, I discovered works by other spiritual teachers, including Wayne Dyer, Eckhart Tolle, and many others. Simultaneously, people with messages that I probably could not have even heard before miraculously showed up on my path, including a friend who reappeared in my life after more than a decade of separation. She already spoke the language I was just starting to learn, and her presence gave me a safe space within which to explore.

The things that I learned in those early days served as a jumping-off point towards an entirely new life. And many of the insights that came will be shared throughout the rest of this book. For now, suffice it to say that my world was blown wide open, and for the first time, I started to get a glimpse of how this blessed Universe works and who I really am.

I refer to this point in my life as a "moment of grace" because it was the priceless gift that I did nothing to earn. My only job was to open and receive.

Grace can be defined as the unmerited favor and love of the Universe, meaning we don't have to work for it. Our worthiness was established when we were born. For a long time, I have described grace as the force that has met me, time and time again, right in the middle of a mess I'd made and refused to leave me there. This could not have been more powerfully true than those initial days of my awakening.

You may have had your own defining moments of grace. Illness, loss of a job, the death of a loved one. There are countless heartaches that open us up. But it's important to remember that the moments of grace of which I speak are characterized, not by the pain that we endured, but by the paradigm shifting insights that often occur because of it. Some are blessed to awaken in other ways that may not be precipitated by pain, but for many, these shifts are born from the depths of despair. The good news, however, is this. We have embarked on a period in the history of our humanity that many call the greatest time of awakening. It's a moment that feels like the Universe is giving us an extra dose of grace as it invites us to open our eyes. With this, the opportunity to simply awaken by choice and not by force has never been more readily available. But how do we even know if we are asleep?

Symptoms of a Sleepy Little World

"It is the nature of the ego to take, and the nature of the spirit to share."
—PROVERB

Do you ever wonder why there is so much pain and polarization in the world? Name a subject. Politics. Racial Injustice. Vaccinations. Abortion. Economic Disparities. Religion. Corporate Greed. If you want to witness a fight, tune into an everyday conversation around any of these topics. Usually, proponents on both sides of any given argument will assume their position and lash out, forcefully, with anyone who disagrees. I am sure you have witnessed a conversation, particularly on social media, deteriorate into a mudslinging match between two deeply passionate souls. It's not uncommon for these dialogues to end with ugly name-calling and even threatening words. Attacks aren't limited to the *beliefs* espoused by the other person. The actual person is attacked. There is no distinction between the beliefs and the person. Why? Because most of us think that we *are* our beliefs.

Many are unable to separate another's beliefs from who they are because they are unable to detach their beliefs from who *they* are. Even good-hearted, well-intentioned people will sometimes turn into dehumanizing demagogues if you trample on what they believe to be true, particularly those ideas that they deem really important, like their moral and religious beliefs.

The same is true for our actions. Never before has what's known as "cancelled culture" been so pronounced. We hold others to a standard of perfection that we could never achieve, and if they fail to meet those expectations, we aim to dismiss the entirety of who they are, unable to separate the person from the perceived offense. It's not, "You did something wrong." It's, "YOU are wrong. The whole of you. And because you are wrong, you must be stamped out. PLUS, You must be stripped of anything that you earned when we thought that you were okay."

At the top of 2020, after returning from a peaceful and life-giving trip to Costa Rica, I was disheartened to see the incredible amount of backlash that Journalist Gayle King was receiving in response to an interview she'd conducted with basketball great Lisa Leslie. She was speaking with Leslie about the tragic loss of basketball icon Kobe Bryant and asked a question about his past that many of his fans considered off-limits. Though he later came to graciously apologize, rapper and entertainer Snoop Dogg led the pack of disgruntled fans who attacked King with threatening, vitriolic words.

I remember being struck by how an entire mass of people, hatefully, stood ready to dismiss Gayle forever because of this one perceived error. She even received death threats. And the irony was the fact that these outraged fans were trying to protect something as nebulous as the "idea" of Kobe's legacy. They were trying to safeguard his image because the belief is, we are *that*.

Our beliefs, our actions, our self-image, our personality, what we have, what we do... all of these things are equated with who we are, and this misidentification is classically known as "the ego." It's that part of us that will launch a full-scale retaliation if it feels threatened in any way.

Our Egos Are Running the Show

The word "ego" is often understood as arrogance or self-admiration, but in the context outlined here, it's much more far-reaching. It presents as the voice in our heads, and it's conditioned by our experiences and the messages that we receive from the world around us. Though it can sometimes feel like the noble protector, "Oh no, I'm being attacked!" it actually causes anxiety, separation, and pain. Often referred to as the little self, the ego is a well-meaning imposter of sorts that keeps you disconnected from who you truly are. And the moment that you begin to consider who you are beyond what you have, do, and think, then you start to awaken.

Recently, my teenaged daughter came to me with a serious look and a serious question. I could tell from her stance that she'd been in deep contemplation about something. She said, "Mom, if I didn't get good grades, and if I didn't play soccer and have my art, would I have any worth?" I felt at least five layers of deep happiness. I know. Strange, right? That I would celebrate a weighty moment in my daughter's life. But the reason I was so delighted to receive her question is because I realized that it represented a powerful doorway to awakening. All of my daughters know where I stand regarding my spiritual beliefs, and they know that I believe that we are eternal beings here to experience the joy of living. But it's not enough for them to know what I believe. The path to owning and accepting our worthiness is a personal one that we must walk alone. It's not enough to have an intellectual or head knowing about who we are. We must develop a heart knowing, and that level of knowing is always preceded by powerful questions.

During that profound moment of grace, when I started to awaken, it was the questions sparked by the resources I was consuming that set me on a new path. Initially, there was nothing more than a subtle, soul-level recognition that they carried truth. Upon reading or hearing certain ideas, something within me simply felt like it had made its way home. And this ignited a firestorm of questions within me. Seeds were planted, and from there, they grew, eventually making their way from my head to my heart.

Prior to that time, my ego had been running the show, completely unchallenged. And now I was discovering that there was a greater me, the real me, that could take the lead to get different results in my life. The weight that I carried as I lashed out at my husband that day was the result of a deep entanglement with my ego. Something would happen, and my emotions would rise or fall depending on whether my ego thought it was a good or bad thing. I was at the mercy of whatever it concluded. If things went my way, my ego would be satisfied. If I won the prize, e.g., the job, the argument, the recognition, the money, etc., it was completely okay. That feeling of being satisfied may have been short-lived, but satisfied, nonetheless. Conversely, if something went awry or against the world according to my ego, then I suffered. It had its own playbook about the "shoulds" and "shouldn'ts" of life. It's how the ego works.

From childhood, we learn rules and customs, how to behave, what to believe, and how we think life should be, and our egos are there taking notes on everything. As we move through life, the ego shows up as the voice in our heads (disguised as "I") reminding us of what has been written. You will know its voice by its need to control, judge, or be accepted. Qualities that are the opposite of the True You or who you really are. And for most of us, it's the voice that dominates the thoughts in our minds.

When I think back to who I was prior to my journey towards awakening, I am downright amazed by the before and after. Truly, my life is the evidence of a greater power. I've always been a decent person with a good heart, but for years, I didn't realize the severity of how I was blocking my own way. I was a "God-fearing, good girl" who aimed to do right in the world. But I also felt powerless and like a victim of the world around me.

The Foundation that Grew My Ego

I enjoyed a good childhood and a strong foundation, but these are some of the experiences that shaped me. I was tall and never thin. There's a picture circling somewhere of me with my kindergarten teacher and a few other kids in my class. I promise you, I'm about the same height as the teacher. Being a tall girl drew attention to me that I didn't want, and this caused me to become self-conscious about my body. I also did well academically, over time becoming known as the smart leader. And when you're a pre-teen/teenager trying to fit in socially, that's not necessarily what you're going for. Smart leaders aren't the ones who get invited to social events.

When I was about 11 or 12, the neighborhood where I lived was smack dab in the middle of the crime scene that was Atlanta, during the Atlanta Missing and Murdered Children era. It was a two-year period where over 28 children and adolescents and a few adults were killed. It was not safe for kids. That was the prevailing message. Every night on television, commercials would run saying to parents, "It's <<insert time>>. Do you know where your children are?" Fear was prime time. One of my classmate's brother was one of the victims, and it was all just too close to home. I'm not sure that the kids of that time ever processed the toll that this took on us. We just grew up and moved on.

Around this time, I was also coping with the very personal stress of witnessing my sweet mom ail. She was ill most of my life, plagued by a host of physical challenges. By the time I was 13, I had learned to take on many household responsibilities, leaning towards adulthood a bit sooner than ideal and reeling from the pain of seeing her suffer. She died when I was 16. I have ten amazing older siblings and a remarkable father who has always done a phenomenal job of taking care of us, but after my mom died, I felt misplaced, like I didn't have a real home. Also, seeing my mom suffer and die led to my having insecurities about my own health, which played a number on my mind for years.

All just stuff. Like the stuff that happens to all of us. But it's stuff that shaped how I moved through the world and that eventually led to insecurities and the prevailing feeling of not being safe and secure. And that feeling would ultimately bleed into many aspects of my life, from my marriage to my finances. Also, I didn't even touch on how societal and cultural programming impacted me, along with the biggie, religion. We'll come back to both of these. For now, I just wanted to give you a sense of the foundational experiences that led to the rise of a looming, reactive, protective, insecure ego that would develop into a shadowy, powerless victim. It was this part of me that was unconsciously leading my life.

When we're spiritually asleep, we are not aware of the fact that the hurt aspects of our personality are in control and calling forth more and more of the same experiences. We cycle through the same patterns that touch on the same wounds over and over because our subconscious mind, a mirror of the ego, is recreating them. It's all that it knows and all that it will know until the light of the soul is invited to shine forth and heal these wounds.

As I entered into adulthood, the themes of not being good enough and not being safe and secure reappeared over and over in countless ways, and for at least 15 years into my adult life, I was unaware that (1) I was stuck in these patterns, and (2) that I had the power and capacity to move beyond them. Our beliefs can translate as conscious and subconscious thoughts that occupy our minds. We know what beliefs are at play based on the results and patterns that we witness in our lives.

One painful pattern that plagued me most of my adulthood centered around money. I mentioned that I have ten siblings. My mom stayed home to care for us and, to my knowledge, never worked outside of the home. My dad was the breadwinner and hustled to provide what we needed. By the time I was born, he worked as an assembly line worker for General Motors, and though he made a decent living, we often had to stretch what came in due to the size of our family. Also, it was not uncommon for him to experience layoffs from time to time, and when he did, things got interesting. I can recall, at least once or twice, going with my mom to a grocery store far away from our neighborhood because she had to use food stamps. Through this, not only did I learn lessons about not having enough, but I also learned to feel ashamed.

When I grew up, I struggled and struggled... and struggled... with money, even after I got married. It seemed we'd always scrape by, barely making it, no matter our income. And oh, the shame. I remember once wanting to go see the Dalai Lama, who was speaking somewhere in Atlanta, and I couldn't go because I didn't have gas money. I was one with shame. Another time, I was with my daughter in a broken-down little ride of a car that had been gifted to us. We were in the parking lot of a restaurant, and when I started the car, I was only able to pull out just a bit before it cut off. It wouldn't budge. We sat in the middle of the parking lot, blocking traffic, and I felt so much humiliation. At one point, a woman yelled at me, and I explained that something was wrong with the car and it wouldn't move. She hurled more expletives, not delivering an ounce of compassion, and with that, even more shame came in.

Honestly, I would have to write another book entirely to talk about all the baggage held and released with regard to money. It has been one of my greatest teachers. And an added reason I struggled was because I didn't understand what was "wrong with me" and why I couldn't move from this place. In my mind, I was a good person, and as I mentioned earlier, I was trying to live right. Why on earth was God punishing me this way? Why wouldn't "he" help me to move beyond this and just send me the money and resources I needed? What about that victorious Christian living? Why couldn't I seem to land there? There's pain, and then there's suffering. I was creating and experiencing both. And now, I understand that this journey is not about being good or not... it's about being asleep or awake.

Symptoms of Being Asleep

By now, you are probably starting to put all of this together. When we are identified with our ego, we are asleep, and when we begin to identify with our true nature, our soul, we start to awaken. Additionally, know that though a moment of grace can occur in an instant and the veil over our eyes starts to lift, the process that begins after that is just that, a process. As I mentioned, it has taken years for me to shift, in a significant way, from where I was before to where I am now, and for sure, the journey continues. My ego is still very much a part of me. The difference is, for the most part, it no longer leads my life. And when it does make its way to the driver's seat, I am now aware enough to recognize it and know when I need to take the keys.

As we move forward, I'd like for you to begin thinking about your own life and the patterns that may be at play. It's important to remember that with the ego, some of the patterning and ways that it presents may not be so obvious. It is its sometimes-subtle nature that makes it difficult to detect. However, once you start to pay attention, you can look out into the world at how others behave and see just how pervasive our egos are in our daily interactions. It doesn't matter how smart, how rich, or how prominent, the ego can easily take the lead in our lives when we are asleep.

Here are just a few ways that you will know your ego is in control:

- ☀ *You feel the need to defend your beliefs.*
- ☀ *You feel threatened when someone misunderstands you.*
- ☀ *You constantly see the flaws in yourself and others.*
- ☀ *You have trouble asking for and receiving help.*
- ☀ *Your sense of security is derived from what you possess.*
- ☀ *You constantly compare yourself to others.*
- ☀ *Your sense of worth is equated with your work in the world.*
- ☀ *You sometimes feel less than when others do well.*
- ☀ *You blame others when things don't go your way.*
- ☀ *You feel superior or inferior to others.*
- ☀ *It's difficult for you to let go.*
- ☀ *It's difficult for you to take criticism and look at yourself objectively.*
- ☀ *You become annoyed or judgmental when others fail to behave the way you think they should.*
- ☀ *You try to prove your worthiness through your actions and behavior.*
- ☀ *You see yourself as a victim.*
- ☀ *You are easily offended.*
- ☀ *You feel triggered in any way.*

Remember, the ego is the part of you that needs to control, judge (yourself, others, and situations), or be accepted. It's the little self. And those last two items on the list above may be the greatest telltale signs of them all, signaling that your ego is in control. Any time that you are *triggered* or *offended*, your ego is in the driver's seat. I know this may be difficult to take in but owning and accepting this is truly the gateway to your power. It's this piece of knowledge that has led to my every conscious breakthrough. Whenever there is an upset within me, my goal is not to try to fix something "out there," i.e., the person or the situation that triggered or offended me, so I will feel better. The goal is to examine myself and shift my thinking about the situation so I can truly be free. Dependence on anything outside of ourselves in order to have peace is relinquishing our power. Further, it's important to emphasize that it does not matter whether you are justly triggered and/or offended or not. That's never the point. Righteous indignation is simply ego disguised as a priest. This is one of the reasons why aspects of some religions feel so heavy and demoralizing, because the ego is walking around in a priestly robe, passing judgments that are justified by holy texts.

The polarization, cancelled culture, the lack of tolerance for those who think and/or behave differently than we do, these things are so prominent in our world because the masses feel justified in their declarations. Our societies are organized based on certain agreed upon principles about how we should conduct ourselves. People shouldn't lie, steal, cheat, hurt and destroy. These are the basics. So, when we believe we have evidence of others operating against these foundational principles, then we feel justified in saying "off with their heads!" Many think we *should* be offended when people behave in certain ways, and if you aren't offended, then you're added to the list of those who need to be fixed.

We fail to realize that if this is our model, then our peace and sense of okayness become dependent on things outside of ourselves. And we also do not realize that the judgment and condemnation that we're leading with is further toxifying the world, no matter how just. Finally, we fail to see that our true nature, which always leans towards love, is being suppressed.

The same is true for those things that trigger and offend us in our personal lives as well. In our day-to-day experiences and in our relationships, whenever we are triggered or offended, our charge is to turn our attention inward to see what egoic beliefs are at play. The world is a reflection of who we are. I will say this no less than a dozen times, I'm sure. In the words of Anais Nin, "We don't see things as they are, we see them as we are." So, the experiences "out there" that trigger us reflect a belief or a wound that we are carrying and indicate that the ego is close by.

What it Means to Awaken

*"Only when the ego has been fully transformed into
a free spirit and the heart is in the lead, we feel complete,
happy and whole. We do not miss anyone or anything.
We feel at home, wherever we go, we live completely
in the now and take life as it comes."*

– VERA INGEBORG

There have been many debates about how the ego should be managed, with some proposing that the goal is to completely dismantle it and others saying that this is impossible. I don't think that the arguments matter. What's important to know is the ego will fade when you place the spotlight of awareness on it. And as you do, you make way for the True You to shine through. This is awakening.

Awakening occurs when we realize we've been operating under conditioning and beliefs that may not be as fixed and solid as we once thought. We were conscious or aware of one reality before something happens (the moment of grace), and then a new possibility is revealed. It's an inner expansion as new depths of our being are revealed. It's the feeling of discovery and revelation as we emerge with an expanded vision about who and what we are.

Spiritual Teacher Eckhart Tolle tells the story of his initial awakening, explaining that one day, in an utter state of misery, with suicidal thoughts nearby, he said to himself, "I cannot live with myself any longer." At that moment, a powerful question came in. He asked, "If I cannot live with myself, who is the self that's saying this?" Suddenly, he was forced to sit with the question of whether there was more than one part of his being. He notes that, eventually, he fell asleep, and the next morning, he had a profound sense of peace that he had not had before. The simple yet powerful question he asked in that moment opened enough spaciousness within him for his true nature to arise. He spent the next several years trying to understand what had happened and eventually discovered wisdom that pointed to the awakening process.

One of the reasons why I love his story so much is because it emphasizes two important things, first, the impact of a powerful question, which we already discussed, and second, the power of awareness.

We have made the path to awakening and healing much more complicated than necessary. Truth is always simple, and once you understand the fundamentals of how things work, then "the work" is simply walking your path (consciously) and maintaining simple practices that deepen your connection with the True You. Awareness, often packaged as mindfulness, is one of those practices.

I like to think of awareness as a spotlight that beams from the mind of God. When we are aware of something, we are observing it in real time, i.e., in the present moment. The present moment, as Eckhart Tolle explains in his highly acclaimed book, "The Power of Now," is a portal to Source or God. The ego lives in one of two places, the past or the future, which is why it often generates negative emotions. We are usually fixated on something that "went wrong," the past, or we have anxiety, or fear, about the future. By contrast, the

True You, the aspect of you that is aligned with God itself (however that's represented to you), resides in the present moment.

This is why learning to still the mind is so valuable. When we are still, we can observe what's happening inside of us, bringing awareness to our inner world. This creates space between our thoughts and our greater sense of knowing and ultimately helps us to see that we are not our thoughts but the consciousness that exists beyond them. That consciousness is the True You, and the True You sees things through the eyes of God.

Eckhart Tolle explains, "The moment you start watching the thinker, a higher level of consciousness becomes activated. You then begin to realize that there is a vast realm of intelligence beyond thought, that thought is only a tiny aspect of that intelligence. You also realize that all the things that truly matter – beauty, love, creativity, joy, inner peace – arise from beyond the mind. You begin to awaken."

So no, there's no need to battle the ego. You only need to walk with the awareness and understanding that it exists. You can even choose to view it as the innocent part of you that only aims to keep you safe. No resisting. No fighting. You only need to love it (through the spotlight of awareness) and reassure it that you've got this. From spiritual teacher Adyashanti, "Meet the ego with absolute love, compassion and patience. Do not indulge it or resist its appearance. Hold it in a loving embrace and let it unravel itself in the stillness of the heart. Let it show you what needs to be healed, the hurt underneath the turmoil. Your presence is the healing agent, your love what allows it to dissolve."

Awakening as a Doorway to Healing

"Your presence is the healing agent..." These words used by Adyashanti are immensely powerful. There is no shortage of pain in the world. And there's no shortage of resources to assist people with managing and healing from their pain. There are behavioral therapies like cognitive behavioral therapy and aversion therapy. There are energy-based therapies like reiki and therapeutic touch. Add to this a self-help industry that's estimated to be a $13 billion dollar industry by 2022. I am here for all of these modalities, and I will forever champion the healers of the world however they show up and whatever modality they choose to offer. I'm one of them. With that, however, I need you to know that the most powerful healing agent you have working on your behalf is your own presence and awareness, which strengthens as you awaken.

It's not uncommon to hear those on a conscious spiritual path speak about the profound healing and transformation they experience as a result of shining the spotlight of awareness on their ego. It's a way of putting some space between yourself and negative emotions that you may be feeling by bringing a non-judgmental awareness to what's happening within you, and it can be a potent and efficient way to dissolve wounds.

Once, I had an argument with my husband that led to an unexpected and profound moment of healing. We'd been at odds with each other, and we were having a conversation about potentially parting ways. Much like most of our arguments during this season of our lives, I argued with an agenda. Not only did I hold my perspective of what was right, but I argued with the distinct expectation that my husband needed to respond according to the script I had running in my mind. If he didn't respond in what I deemed an appropriate way, then my anger and annoyance would intensify.

I can't recall all that was said that night, but I do recall this... in the heat of the moment, as we went back and forth, my husband decided to tune out. While I was still actively arguing my case, he turned his attention towards the television and began watching sports. Are you kidding me!? I was livid. So much so that I felt if I'd had a rope, I would have gone up behind him and choked him! My ego was in full effect. I was hurt, angry, and I was ready for war. Not only was I upset about said subject, but I was also beside myself that he had categorically shut me down by tuning me out. Thankfully, however, I had already started on my path towards awakening. I knew that in order to get different results in my life, I had to try some new strategies.

I'd read about the ego and had learned that in moments like this, instead of lashing out, I needed to go within. And so, I did just that. I went to my bedroom, and I started to take deep breaths. First just to calm down, and then I started intentionally breathing into the place in my body where I felt these raging emotions... in and out, calming my nervous system and focusing within. Then, seemingly out of nowhere, I had a sudden insight. I realized that the knock-down, drag 'em out fight I was having with my husband had nothing to do with him and everything to do with my own sense of safety and security in the world. In that moment, I realized that if we parted, I questioned my ability to take care of myself. It was the equivalent of an instant knowing. There was nothing in that moment but me shining the spotlight of awareness on a wound that I didn't even know that I had. And later, the situation between my husband and me dissolved with relative ease. There was no need for the drama anymore; my soul had shown me what I needed to know. The gift is always for us and never about the other person.

Similarly, in another instance, I once had an intense and vivid dream where I saw a 360 degree view of my life. When I woke up, I immediately knew that the scenes I'd seen in my dream represented a belief that people didn't show up for me in the various aspects of my life. Again, I tuned to where I was feeling this strong emotion of a "lack of support" in my body and realized it was in the center of my chest. By this time, I knew the strategies well, and without even thinking about it, I imagined the healing light of my own awareness, supported by my angels and guides, pouring into that area. And instantly, I felt free from this false belief.

We are guided towards different healing modalities and resources for support as we traverse on our journeys, and as I noted earlier, these can be tremendously helpful. I even have my own sources of support that I tap into when necessary, but as I continue to grow in my understanding of the ways of the Universe, I am convinced that healing does not have to be as complicated as we sometimes make it. I don't believe that we have to chase down childhood wounds and constantly look back to unearth the origin of fear-based beliefs. I believe that oftentimes, we only need to put a bit of space between our presence and the pain, and we do that by focusing our conscious awareness.

That withstanding, I also believe that wherever you are is wherever you are, and it's all okay. We need different things at different points on our journeys, and the lessons for each of us are different. I will always recommend that you seek and find the support that you need, however it shows up and whatever that looks like for you. I tend to appreciate holistic remedies, and once, when I was managing acute back pain, I was speaking with a holistic therapist who said something that really opened my eyes. Essentially, I was in so much pain that she encouraged me to just take the heavy meds that I had been resisting. Her words, "Sometimes you just have to take the medicine to interrupt the cycle of pain and give you what you need in the moment. From there, once you are settled enough, you can chart a path in the best direction for you." It's all okay.

It's All Happening for You

"Everything that seemingly happens externally is occurring
in order to trigger something within us, to expand us and
take us back to who we truly are."
– ANITA MOORJANI

The world is a projection of our inner thoughts. Again, as within, so without. This is an unfailing, organizing principle of the Universe. And its deliverance to us is itself an act of grace. Because of this principle, as I noted before, we can look at our lives and know what beliefs (both conscious and subconscious) are at play. If we are experiencing lack, then somewhere within us is lack consciousness. If we're experiencing feelings of neglect or abandonment, then somewhere within us are beliefs that are calling forth this experience. The world is indeed a mirror, and it is constantly reflecting back to us those beliefs that are active within us. Accordingly, in the classic, "As a Man Thinketh," author James Allen writes, "Circumstance does not make the man; it reveals him to himself."

This is a gift. If we want to know what needs to be healed within us, we only need to look at the circumstances of our lives. It's this fundamental truth that has led to the understanding that life isn't happening *to* us; rather, it's happening *for* us. This is our point of power. When something hurts, we don't spend our energy and focus trying to fix the circumstance so we will feel better. Instead, we understand that we are hurting because there is an aspect of our consciousness that is creating that experience or circumstance due to either our conscious or subconscious beliefs. This means that we aren't dependent on anything outside of ourselves for our own healing and peace. Furthermore, it means that instead of fighting against people and situations that have caused us pain, we can shift our perspective and extend gratitude for the revelations they bring. Spiritual teacher Colin Tipping calls this "radical forgiveness," explaining that we can reframe our stories and consider that there may be a larger purpose or gift behind the experience, there to illuminate an aspect of our own consciousness that's ready to be healed. Referring to reframing as stage four of a multi-staged process, Tipping says, "Stage four asks us to be willing to look at the possibility that there might be divine purpose behind everything that happens, and that what happened to make us feel victimized was actually what our 'spiritual self' had wanted for its growth, and that our spiritual intelligence had created the situation for us."

Once I truly got this, everything changed. I was no longer a victim of any story that I was telling myself and no longer warring with the world. The world had nothing to do with any pain that I felt; it was merely showing me my tender places so I could choose whether or not I was ready to offer them up to be healed. The rule of thumb? If it's a situation that stings even a little, then there's a belief to uncover somewhere. The pain shows us what we need to see, not out there, but within ourselves.

Again, this is good news because we don't need the world to adjust in order to be free. One example of this from my own life centers around the issue of race. For a long time, I would have the experience of going into certain types of stores and being ignored by sales associates. These would be stores that leaned towards higher-end products, with a predominantly white clientele. It would almost be without fail. I'd walk in and not be greeted. Or the sales associate would look *beyond* me to ask another white patron if they needed help. It would make me livid. And many times, I would point it out to the sales associate or manager, voicing my "justified" frustration. Am I invisible? Are they *all* racists?

And then, as I started to awaken and learn some of the principles I'm sharing with you, I learned to pause and take a look within. Were there some hidden beliefs that were fueling these experiences? As I tuned in, I realized that, indeed, I was unconsciously calling these experiences to me based on my conscious (and unconscious) expectations and because of my own feelings of inadequacy and unworthiness. As I mentioned earlier, one of the things I struggled with was money and a lack, and at a point, I realized I was entering into these stories with my own insecurities front and center. I was the one who questioned whether or not I belonged.

Over time, I was able to heal this wound, and I did so simply by owning and accepting responsibility for these experiences. The sales associates who had responded to me in ways that triggered me were only pawns in my own carefully crafted story and staged production. And believe me, before I started to awaken, it was quite the masterpiece. Full of drama and evidence of wrongdoing. Years later, I am in a totally different place, and the experiences that I have when out in the world and entering spaces like those described are predominantly pain-free. I consistently meet amazing, helpful, friendly people of all hues and persuasions, not because they changed, but because I did.

The world around us is truly a platform for our own spiritual unfolding. Things aren't happening "to us," they're happening "for us," to awaken us to who we truly are. Once we learn to OWN our experiences, then we can begin to rescript our stories and awaken to new possibilities. And as we do, a whole world starts to open around us.

What to Expect Upon Awakening

Once you start to tune to your inner world, things will start to shift. It's certain. As you focus on growing the True You, the world around you will have to change as it starts to reflect the emerging shifts within you. One of my favorite spiritual teachers, Wayne Dyer, is famously known for saying, "Change the way that you look at things and the things you look at will change." As our beliefs and perspectives start to change, the world around us changes too.

This truly is something to get excited about. Because this is how we begin to create our own heaven on earth experience. Regardless of what's happening in the larger world around you, your personal world can be filled with peace, love, and joy. And to the degree that this powerful dynamic grows within you, then that goodness reverberates in the world and shifts it too.

With this, however, it's also wise to understand that awakening does not immediately lead to all sunshine and rainbows. Contrast and challenges will still come, but how you respond to them will be the difference-maker. If you lead with the belief and knowing that "everything serves" and "it's all happening FOR you," then you will bring less resistance to the situation and position yourself to receive its associated gifts. Topping the list of these gifts will be knowledge of self and knowledge of others. Also, as your external world shifts in response to the emerging True You, then oftentimes, this means that those structures that are currently in place may have to fall away or be repositioned as new things come in. Sometimes, we cling to those things that are familiar, like the job or even certain relationships, but as we evolve, those things must change to reflect who and where we are on our journey, OR they must fall away.

This is why we must learn to hold things loosely and without attachment. We typically have our thoughts and ideas about how we think things should unfold, but awakening means giving our souls permission to take the lead. And our souls have a much higher perspective of what changes need to happen in order for us to advance on our paths. I cannot tell you how many times I initially felt resistance to something that turned out to be the biggest gift. So now, I constantly remind myself that things are always working out for me, even when I don't immediately see how. For the longest time, my power word was "believe." The early stages of awakening were an intense faith walk. As I learned more and more about how the Universe works, I had to train myself to hold on and *believe* that "all is well." Over time, after several years, that believing shifted into "knowing," which represented the point at which I had sufficient evidence that things are indeed always working out for me.

I'm sharing this because I want you to know that there will be plenty of times, particularly as you advance through the other stages of the transformation model, i.e., Align, Flow, and Love, when you question everything. Have heart, allow yourself to be where you are at any given moment. And then, when it's time, just get back up again. At times, you may even question whether the desire to get back up will ever return. It will. Any gains you achieve in growing your level of awareness or consciousness cannot be loss. We may have moments when we feel disconnected, but eventually, we are able to tune once again to the voice of our soul and find our way. I've also noticed that the valley moments are not as deep nor elongated as I grow in and by grace.

So, know that periods of frustration and impatience... common and to be expected. Shifts in relationships... common and to be expected. As you grow, there will be those who will grow with you and others who will choose to distance themselves. You will also make the choice to distance yourself in relationships that may not fit anymore or see challenging relationships with new eyes. I encourage you to trust the process and allow things to unfold as they need to. And know that this list may extend to any aspect of your life, from your career to your finances. Whatever unfolds, know that (1) external changes come with internal shifts, (2) sometimes the old must be stripped away before the new can come in, and (3) no matter how it appears, things are always working out for you. Indeed, everything serves, and all is well.

Awaken Power Tools

Awakening is about slowing down, taking a long, deep, and introspective look at our lives, and inviting grace to open our eyes to the truth of who we are. It's about remembering. And there are many things you can do to support the awakening process, regardless of where you are on your journey.

The power tools that I offer here are tried and true. I have found that my soul guides me towards what I need, and sometimes I'll find myself engaged in practices before I even realize they are "a thing." As we learn to quiet our minds, we can more clearly hear the voice of our souls. You should also know that the tools in this and other sections are also derived from ancient wisdom. I love knowing that many of our greatest spiritual traditions and religions point to many of the same tools. As I've said before, Universal truth is Universal truth.

As you move along your path, you are invited to use them as a part of your own spiritual practice, routinely or whenever you feel the need for a boost. Some have become staples for me, and they are non-negotiable. I find that I need to partake of them consistently to stay grounded and steady. Some, however, I will flow in and out of depending on my specific needs. Find what works for you.

Power of Stillness

*"You are never more essentially, more deeply,
yourself than when you are still."*
– ECKHART TOLLE

Imagine a lake and the trees and other elements in the environment that surround it. When the winds are high, or something in it is causing motion along its surface, what does the reflection of the surrounding area look like in that water? The image is distorted, right? What happens to the image when the water is still? Yep, you're right again. When the water is still, the image is clear. Well, just like water, when we are still, our perceptions are clear. We can hear and see more clearly. Stillness serves us because it creates space for us to find our way to the truth of who we are.

If you're like most, your life is probably moving at a pretty rapid rate most of the time. It's a part of our culture. As a matter of fact, busyness is often viewed as a sign of how important someone is. And without even realizing it, we unconsciously buy into it. Also, sometimes, we have a subconscious fear of slowing down because we don't want to see what's really going on in our lives. The Swiss Psychologist Carl Jung once said, "Man will do anything to avoid facing his own soul." And yet, there's nothing to fear and so much to gain. Sometimes we fear that if we tune to the voice of our soul, we will be led towards a life of spiritual renunciation. I assure you that any path that your soul leads you towards will be paved with joy, peace, happiness, and love, for these are the languages of the soul.

So, don't be afraid of stillness, befriend it. Know that your awakening is intricately tied to your capacity to sense the quiet, sacred, expansive world within you. As you learn to slow your pace and quiet your mind, stillness will soon become a non-negotiable part of your days because it will feed you so.

Power of Patterns

"There's truth in patterns but it's the kind of truth that's hard to accept - the truth we don't always see because we're not always looking."
– ADAM GNADE

As a Career Coach, people come to me, oftentimes, because they are challenged by some aspect of their career, and they want out. They may have a bully for a boss. They may have a disrespectful co-worker who they can no longer tolerate. Or maybe they have been overlooked for a promotion they felt they deserved. Whatever the case, one of the first things I'll do is ask enough questions to determine if what they are experiencing is something they've dealt with before. One time? We need to explore other possibilities. Two times? A theme is probably developing. Three times? Indeed, we have ourselves a pattern. It's also possible that the pattern could be playing out beyond the walls of their career. For example, maybe they have a bully for a boss and a bully for a husband and a bully for a mom. Patterns. It's usually at this point that I will explain that there's an opportunity and a gift brewing somewhere, and we need to take time to figure out what it is. I also explain that the moment is not just about moving from one job to another because until the root issue is identified and healed, then they will just continue to meet the same people over and over wherever they are.

As we start to awaken, it's imperative that we take time to contemplate the patterns at play in our lives. If there are situations that you find yourself in repeatedly, this is not random, and it's not luck. We create with both our conscious and subconscious minds, and we know what we're creating based on the circumstances of our lives. Are you constantly attracting needy people into your life? Do you always end up in relationships that seem to play out the same way? Are your contributions consistently overlooked at work?

Are you always struggling to get ahead? It's important to seek out these types of patterns, not to feel shame, but to reclaim your power. There's a common saying that "You cannot heal what you cannot see." Once we become aware of these patterns, we can offer them up and ask for divine guidance and support to heal. As I mentioned before, simply putting the spotlight of awareness on it and creating some space around it will absolutely move you in the right direction. Awareness puts you in the seat of power.

Power of Presence

"In any moment, no matter how lost we feel, we can take refuge in presence and love. We need only pause, breathe, and open to the experience of aliveness within us. In the wakeful openness, we come home to the peace and freedom of our own natural awareness."
– TARA BRACH

The final tool that will serve you as you awaken is the "Power of Presence." Presence is the art of being fully in the now. When you are present, you are alert and open to hear and see what's happening in you and around you. And as you are probably already sensing, presence is intricately tied to stillness, as stillness is a gateway to presence.

As I mentioned earlier, for most of us, before we start on a conscious path, our minds run the show, and they take us wherever they choose without much interference. We're at the mercy of whatever our egos are fixated on in the moment. If you stop to think about your thinking, if you're like most, you will probably realize that your mind is like a monkey, jumping from tree to tree, i.e., from one thing to the next, without pause. Apart from being exhausting, what this does is keep you away from the present moment, which is the only place where you can tune to the voice of your soul. Stress, worry, fear, regret... none of these things can exist in the present moment. Because when you are fully present, you are attuned to each moment as it arises, simply observing it without judgment.

To cultivate presence, you have to do things that will help you to stop the incessant stream of mental chatter that typically occupies the mind. The best way to do this is to be fully with and focused on whatever you're doing in any given moment. For example, if you're washing dishes, be with the process fully. Any time you notice your mind wandering, come back to washing the dish in front of you. You can also do this with activities such as walking or exercising. Be fully present, not allowing your thoughts to live in the past or the future.

One of the easiest and most powerful ways to practice being present is by consciously tuning to your breath, breathing in and out with your gentle focus, and returning to this whenever your mind drifts away. Initially, it may feel difficult and even uncomfortable to do this, but with practice, you can absolutely strengthen this muscle, and as you do, the True You will illuminate more and more.

Here are some practices that will create spaciousness in your life and support these three power tools:

- ❀ Sit quietly and reflect.
- ❀ Take naps and rest more.
- ❀ Practice taking conscious breaths throughout the day.
- ❀ Turn off your technology for dedicated periods of time.
- ❀ Spend time in nature or with animals. Nature carries a presence that invites stillness.
- ❀ Indulge in reading books with content that make you feel settled, peaceful, and grounded.
- ❀ Add simple activities like drinking tea into your day, without external distractions.
- ❀ Engage in activities that cultivate stillness, like prayer, meditating, chanting, and yoga.
- ❀ Create a private sanctuary with things that calm and ground you, e.g., crystals, candles, prayer beads, etc.

☀ Go for meditative walks and observe things around you.

☀ Bring your conscious attention to what's happening in your body, particularly when you're feeling a strong emotion. Notice where it lives in your body and breath into it.

☀ Tune into something rhythmic like the hum of a fan or the flicker of a candle.

Awaken Reflective Questions

1. *What surfaces for you when you ask, "Who am I?" How do you define yourself? Who are you beyond the roles that you carry?*

2. *Do you feel that you are living your own truth? What would it look like to be more fully you?*

3. *On average, what percentage of your days are you really present for?*

4. *When do you feel most like yourself?*

5. *Is the public you different from the private you? If so, which one is really you?*

6. *How important is what others think of you?*

7. *What patterns have you noticed in your life? What situations do you find yourself in repeatedly?*

8. *How can you cultivate more stillness and presence in your life? What practices are you willing to commit to?*

Awaken Soul Qualities

As we move through each of the four phases of transformation, there are certain soul qualities (among many) that are unlocked within us. These soul qualities are an inherent part of our natural essence, but as our experiences and cultural conditioning strengthen the ego, they fade to the background. As you use your tools and consciously tune to the voice of your soul, these soul qualities will begin to flourish once again. I name them because it can be helpful to understand what they are and how they present. Also, intentionally working to cultivate them will support your transformation, as these qualities will strengthen your connection with both your true self and others. The soul qualities unlocked during the awakening phase are self-awareness, authenticity, and vulnerability.

Self-Awareness

*"Until you make the unconscious conscious, it will direct
your life and you will call it fate."*
– CARL JUNG

Self-awareness is having the capacity to look within and to know oneself intimately. Simply stated, it's understanding who you are. It's having a clear perception of your strengths, weaknesses, thoughts, beliefs, values, motivators, emotional triggers, and more. It's also having a clear understanding of how others perceive and respond to you.

As you develop your self-awareness, you will strengthen your capacity to choose your response to situations, thereby being less reactive. It is the key to personal mastery and can positively affect all aspects of your life, from your relationships to your career.

The power tools for Awaken, stillness, patterns, and presence, unlock self-awareness because they create space for you to tune to your inner world.

Authenticity

*"Don't try to be beautiful. Just be real, and that is already
beautiful enough."*
– JEFF FOSTER

You were born as a unique expression of the divine. Christian theology explains that we are made in the image of God, but I don't think we've even begun to grasp what that truly means. The Universe is a symphony of exquisite and extraordinary things to behold. It's as if it challenged itself to expand and reveal itself in as many magnificent ways as possible. It unfolds as an infinite stream of its own beauty, reflected in different ways, and each replication, from the bird in the tree to you, is one of those creative expressions. And just as each bird makes this world a more lovely place, just by being what it was born to be, so do you. Your personality, your quirks, your sense of style, the way you speak, your unique gifts, your way of dancing with the world, all of these things contribute to the universal symphony to make the sound that it creates perfect and glorious. And in the absence of you contributing those things as intended, something very special goes missing in the music that the rest of us came to enjoy. Further, the reality is, you will end up moving through this world and this life, never really feeling satisfied and fulfilled because you are suppressing the very aspects of your soul that you came here to express. Out of all of nature, we are the only ones who try to shapeshift into something that we are not.

Being authentic is about embracing and expressing your uniqueness, affirming your own truths, and aligning with your truest soul's expression. It's a willingness to own your humanity and acknowledge your imperfections. It is acceptance, allowance, and an appreciation of who and what you are. Some people think that being authentic is about unleashing your "no holds barred," uninhibited self. However, being authentic is NOT about just showing up as you are without self-management and self-modulation. The small, egoic self is not your authentic self. Your authentic self is your best self. Your authentic self is the True You.

Vulnerability

"I think one's relationship with one's vulnerability is a very delicate and precious relationship. Most people try to hide, disguise that vulnerability, and in doing that, you, I think, diminish a great source of power."
– PHILIP SCHULTZ

Vulnerability is very much connected to authenticity in that authenticity can only be realized if we have the courage to express it and show who we really are. Vulnerability represents that willingness to share your true nature with others. It's the willingness to allow others to see what is real in you and to find resonance with the part of you that is connected to God itself. Some believe that vulnerability is a sign of weakness, but nothing could be further from the truth. Vulnerability is strength. It's a quiet courage that says, "Yes, I am strong enough to risk emotional exposure and show you my soul."

We avoid vulnerability for fear of being judged, but there is nothing within you that warrants living in the shadows. Furthermore, those who would judge you are doing so from their own small, egoic selves. And when you stand with your full "soul on deck" posture and dare to allow others to see your true beauty, then you spark that something in them that yearns to be equally free.

So much of the world feels like a façade. We are craving genuine connections. But these genuine connections can only become our lived reality if we dare to remove the masks that prevent our souls from shining through. There is a certain welcomed innocence that comes with vulnerability. There's no pretense... just you, just me, just us, being who we are.

PART II:
ALIGN

Soul Rising

*"When you examine the lives of the most influential people
who have ever walked among us, you discover one thread that
winds through them all. They have been aligned first with
their spiritual nature and only then with their physical selves."*
—Albert Einstein

It was the fall of 2006 when I took the tumble down the stairs that kickstarted my awakening. My back was so severely injured that I was mostly confined to bed for about three months. And it was during that time that I studied and began to see that there was much more to this world than I knew. At the time, I was working with one of the best chiropractors in Atlanta, and he'd advised that my lack of progress with his services suggested that a more conventional medical intervention may be necessary. With that, I felt I had no other options but to pursue the path that my medical doctor was recommending, so I scheduled surgery for January the following year.

What I didn't fully understand at the time was the fact that the pain in my back represented an enormous amount of emotional pain that I had been carrying for years. Though I believe that illness can sometimes result for other reasons, it is commonly held that the stress of emotional pain and struggle, left unchecked, will eventually manifest into physical pain. And at that time, it felt as if every false belief, worry, heartache, insecurity, and misunderstanding had landed right at the base of my spine. It had gripped me so severely that I could barely stand, and when I did, I was positioned in a near 90-degree angle and walked like a 90-year-old woman in severe pain.

But the miraculous occurred. The awakening process, by definition, includes a whole lot of purging and releasing. One of the books I was reading at the time was Sarah Ban Breathnach's "Something More: Excavating Your Authentic Self," and I recall doing work, guided by the book, that truly felt like an archeological dig. I was in search of myself, and though the true me was buried beneath a whole lot of gooky layers, I was finding pieces of her. And it was as if with each layer that was removed, a tiny bit of pressure was relieved from my back.

That's what was happening in the spiritual. In the physical, I'd started to try holistic remedies while I waited for surgery, and one really helpful therapy that I "stumbled upon" was castor oil packs. It involved soaking a piece of unbleached wool in pure castor oil and applying it to my back with heat. A godsend! These treatments were soothing and powerful, so much so that by January, I'd gotten so much better that I was able to cancel the surgery.

Since then, I've grown to understand that just as the emotional stress and pain precede the physical ailment, the releasing of the same stress and pain will oftentimes lead to the physical breakthrough. Some may look at how things unfolded and simply credit the castor oil pack as being the catalyst for my healing. However, I am well aware of the potency in the spiritual work that I was doing simultaneously. We are multifaceted, whole beings, and our minds, bodies, and spirits are intricately connected, I believe, in ways that we are only beginning to understand.

In "You Can Heal Your Life," which I highly recommend, renown author and lecturer Louise Hay explains how limiting beliefs and ideas can lead to illness and how healing can come from changing these thought patterns. She says, "If we are willing to do the mental work, almost anything can be healed." In the book, she includes a directory of ailments and outlines the emotional causes that may have contributed to them. She also provides corresponding affirmations that can support healing. Hay's own life included evidence of the work she espoused, having healed from cancer using the principles she taught. She lived to be a vibrant and healthy 90-year-old, leaving this earthly plane by drifting away in her sleep. Healthy, here, happy, gone. Truly an exemplary model.

Finding My Way

Once I regained my health, I returned to my spa party business, but I knew that things had to shift. I was keenly aware of the fact that my back could no longer withstand the heavy-duty physical nature of the work, and more importantly, my soul was inching towards fulfilling a purpose that I was only beginning to understand. As I was healing, emotionally and spiritually, there was a part of me that knew that what I was learning was not just for me. Helping others to grow and evolve was written in my soul's blueprint. And as I started to awaken, this part of me began to come alive. I went through an intense stage where I journaled and documented everything. The journaling helped me to work things out in my own heart and soul, and it also helped me to make connections and understand the process that I was going through. And immediately, I wanted to share what I was learning with others.

One of the first things I did was attempt to incorporate a personal development component into our spa party offerings. Our services were designed for women and girls, and now I wanted to offer more than just beauty treatments to pamper their bodies; I wanted to offer experiences that would grow their minds. I tweaked packages here and there and added new spins on the work that we were doing, but I just couldn't find the right rhythm.

A year or so prior to that time, I'd been featured in a few media outlets, including Ebony and Southern Living Magazines, for my work as an entrepreneur. The publicity seemed to take on a life of its own, and in 2007, I was invited to be on the Rachael Ray Show. Actress Angela Bassett and her husband and actor Courtney Vance were the headliners for the particular show that I was on, and it all truly felt like a dream. I even naively announced that my company was planning to franchise. I had no real clue about how to make the business work, and there was one fundamental problem. I wasn't making any real money. Most of what we were earning was going to payroll or back into the business. By the summer of 2008, I made the decision to shut it down. I needed to direct my attention towards something else.

In all of this, my soul was steadily rising. We are born into this world with a particular mission and purpose in tow, and our souls will always guide us towards the path of least resistance to get us where we need to be. At this time, the desire to share what I was learning with others was steadily mounting, and I yearned to find an outlet to express this desire. Simultaneously, I was going back and forth with my husband as we wrestled over the need for me to find work that would support our household.

At some point during all of this, I'd created my first vision board. A vision board is a collage that serves as a visual representation of our hopes and desires in different areas of our lives. There are different ways to approach it, but with my first one, I simply found images that I was attracted to in magazines and added them to my board. The guidance I'd received was not to spend too much time pondering the images or trying to understand them, but instead, to just go with the flow and trust the process.

I can't recall all of the details of that first board, but one thing that I distinctly remember was seeing the term "life coach" in Oprah's magazine. I didn't even know what it meant, but it was interesting and appealing for some reason, so I cut it out and added it to my board.

When the Soul Carves Out the Plan

In order to meet my husband's request to land a steady job, I returned to what I knew, which was higher education. I'd previously worked as a student affairs administrator for several years and felt confident that I could land a position in my area of expertise, Residence Life. But my soul had a different plan.

I applied for a position as Director of Residence Life at Wesleyan College, a women's college in Georgia, and I was invited to interview. I felt pretty sure that I would get the position until the Vice President for Student Affairs called me with a different idea. She said that she'd opted to hire someone for the Residence Life position who she thought would be a better fit, and wanted to know if I would be interested in assuming the role of Director of Career Services. What!? I was confused and maybe even a bit annoyed, and so I politely declined her offer.

A week or so later, I was sitting talking to my husband about how things had transpired, and I asked him if he thought I'd made the right decision to decline. My husband is nothing if he isn't direct. He said, "No." Without hesitation, I immediately ran upstairs and emailed the VP to see if the position was still open. She said that my timing was perfect, and indeed it was. I accepted the offer, and thankfully, my soul won this round.

The new post was the perfect position for me. I loved my team. I loved the students. And I loved having a new playground that would allow me to guide others towards realizing their hopes and dreams.

While this was brewing, I was also starting to try my hand at training teams. My dear friend, Ulisa Bowles, who champions me in ways that amaze me, saw possibilities and potential in me that I'm not sure that I fully realized myself, not back then. We'd worked together at Clark Atlanta University for a number of years, attending grad school there as well. In my various roles, I'd trained both students and professional staff, and perhaps because of what she witnessed there, she invited me to do some work with a team she was now leading at another institution. It was my first independent training gig. A full day in the arena, teaching, sharing, and loving on the participants. I was hooked.

By the fall of 2009, through a path that truly seemed to find me and with money that miraculously appeared, I enrolled in a program to gain a certification as a Life Purpose and Career Coach, Life Coach, and Spiritual Coach. That such a perfect program existed still amazes me to this day. By January of 2010, I was fully certified. The position, the certification, the training that I did for Ulisa's team, these were all stepping-stones towards my living purpose and the rising of the true me.

Aligning with Purpose

As we awaken and grow in consciousness, our souls will begin to take their rightful place. And the way that we serve is one of the ways that this is reflected. We all have a yearning to discover our purpose. The yearning itself is the soul's attempt to communicate with us and lead us towards our highest path. The restlessness, the longing for something more, this will gnaw at our hearts until we open to what's wanting to emerge. Purpose pulls and calls us all. The challenge is we often singularly associate purpose with our work in the world when it is actually much broader than this.

The easiest way to think of it is to see purpose as having two dimensions. We can call these an inner purpose and an outer purpose. Your inner purpose is to align with your best and highest self, what we are calling the "True You," and to joyfully live from that place. Your soul is an eternal being that's on its path as an ever-unfolding, beautiful expression of the divine. And you, in your humanity, came here to partner with your soul to explore this world and witness its beauty. As you honor this, the depths of your inner world grow in its magnificence, and life becomes a sweet and joyful adventure.

Your outer purpose, then, is to serve the world from this powerful place of soul alignment. And though it does involve using your natural talents and gifts, in terms of your outward expressions and offerings, it also includes the glorious act of simply being who you are. Purpose is not limited to our actions; it also includes our "being." You, expressing all dimensions of your soul's splendor, from your unique gifts and abilities to your unique brand of creativity, wisdom, humor, beauty, and joy... all of this is a part of you boldly living out your purpose.

Your soul's expression is unique to you, and the world needs you freely radiating your own brand of beauty to complete the harmonics of our collective musical symphony. So, as you free yourself to be yourself OR *be* yourself to *free* yourself, you win because you will satisfy the yearnings of your soul. And the rest of us win because you will be gracefully beautifying your corner of the world.

Know that if you are on a path to unlock your purpose, to find true fulfillment, you must do the work of tending to both your inner and outer purpose. It's the most powerful way to move towards authentic success. And truly, the secret gift that we can easily miss is this... as you do the deep inner work, the outer work will unfold on its own accord. It must. The path of awakening will land you where you need to be. The right opportunities, the right resources, all that you need will meet you in divine right timing. This is certainly demonstrated by the twists and turns in my own career. Director of Career Services. That position was nowhere on my radar. But that was okay because my soul knew that it was the perfect next step for me. And though I almost self-sabotaged and got in my own way, the path still unfolded, which illuminates another beautiful aspect of how this all works. I believe that if I had continued to resist the career services opportunity, then my soul would have simply led me to another path to get what I needed at that time. We can't get it wrong. We can only cause unnecessary suffering for ourselves along the way.

Assuming Your Role
as a Creator

"The closer you come to knowing that you alone create the
world of your experience, the more vital it becomes for you
to discover just who is doing the creating."
– ERIC MICHA'EL LEVENTHAL

While I served in the position at Wesleyan College, interesting things were brewing in my household. I mentioned before that as we grow and expand spiritually, those we are in a relationship with will grow with us, or the dynamics of the relationship will shift. This happens in friendships and partnerships of all kinds, including marriage. It's a common tale. So, I consider myself most fortunate that my awakening journey has very much been in tandem with my husband's. It's almost as if from the moment I stepped onto my conscious path, he was standing right beside me, stepping onto his own. This has been invaluable to me. Though his path has been very much his own, the Universe has created this beautiful, blended journey between the two of us where we have been able to share in the new language of the soul that we've been learning. So, in some ways, this story is as much a story about "our" unfolding as it is "mine."

By 2011, in our attempts to grow ourselves, we had both consumed an enormous amount of information. We explored the works of those we'd both declare as our favorite teachers, such as Eckhart Tolle and Wayne Dyer, but there was a good bit of divergence in our journeys as well. I became a fan of teachers like Vietnamese Monk Thich Nhat Han and speaker Dr. Sue Morter, while my husband, Willis, studied more formal bodies of wisdom such as "A Course in Miracles," The I-Ching, and the Bhagavad Gita. This made our discoveries even richer and more interesting to explore. And without question, walking in a similar direction fueled our growth and undeniably saved our marriage... many times.

We were both excited and on fire about what we were learning, so much so that we were eager to apply these spiritual insights into our work. I was still in my role as Director of Career Services at Wesleyan College, and I enjoyed it, but I yearned to be free to do my own thing in my own way. I'd started a business on the side offering coaching and training, and by this time, I'd had enough experience (or so I thought) where I wanted to do it full time.

Willis is a passionate and accomplished educator with a love for students that is incredible to witness. He has long been a champion of educational reform, and as he grew spiritually, he concluded that students, parents, and teachers would be best served if we consciously incorporated ancient wisdom and spiritual truth into how we educate our kids. This led him to write a book called "Igniting Purpose: A Spiritual Approach to Educating Our Children," and he was excited to share his ideas with the world. Working in education had become tremendously taxing for him because he felt that the system overemphasized testing and standardization. In essence, for him, there was too much focus on "teaching to the test" and not enough focus on honoring the brilliance in all kids, even when disguised.

So, with both of our souls stirring, we met up one day in a conversation that basically went something like this:

Willis: *"I can't do this any longer. I feel really passionate and guided to pursue a different path. I want to share my book and ideas with the world and impact the next generation of teachers. I'm quitting my job."*

Me: *"I feel equally passionate about the work that I want to do. I have a plan that will start us off on a solid foundation financially and allow me to pursue my work full time. I'm quitting my job too."*

Did I mention that we were both on fire?

Our families thought we were nuts, and our girls still remind us of this time that I sometimes refer to as the "desert years." We both fell flat on our faces. Nothing worked out as planned. There was no financial cushion, and initially, we felt betrayed by the Universe. Both of us felt strongly that our decision to leap was divinely inspired and guided. As such, we just couldn't understand why we didn't soar to become America's next success story. It took years to recover, spiritually, emotionally, and financially. In some sense, some of the remnants are still being cleaned up. But I've come to understand that our decisions were indeed divinely inspired, though they didn't yield the outcome we expected. For me, these desert years were about learning how to truly be the creator that I was born to be.

Our Souls Care Most About Our Spiritual Evolution

As I mentioned before, we have an inner purpose and an outer purpose, and we experience authentic success when our outer purpose flows from our alignment with our inner purpose. I was eager to focus on the outer purpose, and I made progress in many ways, but my agenda was not the same as my soul's agenda. The greater goal, as outlined by my soul, was to help me to grow as I continued to awaken, not to bypass "go" on my way to Park Avenue. If things had unfolded the way that we both expected, I would have missed layers and layers of inner growth. The veil had started to lift from my eyes, but my vision was far from clear. I'd learned a lot about how the Universe works, but I had not yet lived the concepts I'd learned. And head knowing and heart knowing are two completely different things.

The desert years brought an abundance of opportunities for me to see how I was shaping my world. Though I had grown quite a bit, I still carried lots of beliefs and insecurities that prevented me from truly being free. Furthermore, all the experiences that landed at my door were of my own creation, but I was far from really understanding how. It is said that "7" is the number of completion, which is represented in many faiths and traditions. So, perhaps it's not a coincidence that this chapter of my life lasted about seven years. It was the space in time when I became intimately acquainted with the laws of the Universe and how they applied to my life.

With my initial awakening, I had glimpsed my power, or at least I was intrigued by the notion that I had it. But now it was time to truly experience it. And so, as I learned, I applied what I learned, and I grew. Over time, I got to the point where I was willing to own it all. I realized first-hand how my choices affected the outcomes I experienced.

Now, I'm able to share what I've learned with you and my clients with an unshakeable confidence and resolve. My commitment to you is this—if you steadily apply the principles I'm about to share, your life will change. This will not happen overnight, and you will still experience challenges, for challenges are an inherent part of life. But with dedicated spiritual practice, you will soon realize your power to create your own heaven on earth experience, which can only come from alignment with your soul.

The Keys to Alignment

There are two aspects of your being, your personality (humanity) and your soul (divinity), which is an extension of God or the Universe. When we're born, we show up as these pure radiant beings who are fully aligned with the soul of who we are. We only know love. However, over time, our egoic nature rises as a response to painful experiences and cultural conditioning, and we start to think in ways that make us feel disconnected from our divine nature. The word "feel" should be emphasized here because, in truth, we are never disconnected from the deeper aspects of who we are. It's possible, however, for our conscious minds to be so attuned to fear-based thought patterns that we can barely hear the whispers of our souls, which always stand ready to take the lead in our lives. Our personalities live in our minds while our souls live in our hearts. If we want to live the lives we are meant to live, we must learn how to align our heads and our hearts... or our personalities and our souls. And to do this, we must repattern our thoughts.

Our personalities are meant to operate in service of the soul, meaning our souls were always meant to take the lead in our lives. However, because of fear-based patterns that emerged, this was reversed, and the voice of our soul was dampened as the rational mind took the lead. Now, particularly in the Western world, we appreciate and honor those things that we can understand and know with our physical senses, through our rational mind, and we discredit our intuitive knowing, i.e., the voice of the soul. Einstein is credited with saying, "The intuitive mind is a sacred gift and the rational mind is a faithful servant. We have created a society that honors the servant and has forgotten the gift." Said differently, we honor the personality, and we've forgotten the soul. In order for our lives to flow as intended, we must learn to yield to the original plan where the soul leads and guides.

No one illuminates this more beautifully and creatively than Gary Zukav in his highly acclaimed book, "The Seat of the Soul." Gary explains, "Every fleet of ships that sails has a mothership; one ship that knows where all of them are going and sets the direction for all of those ships to sail. This doesn't mean that the mothership determines what happens on each of the other ships in the fleet. Life on one of the ships might be mostly pleasant. On yet another ship, it might be mostly unpleasant. Now imagine the mothership is the biggest ship you can imagine, it's a city afloat, magnificent. Now imagine that the rest of the ships aren't really ships, but they're little boats. The mothership is your soul and you are one of the little boats. The mothership knows why you are in the water. You may not know all of the time. The mothership knows why you encounter storms. Your job, while you have the awesome privilege of being a little boat, is to learn how to sail in the same direction as your mothership. Because you can choose and create anything you want, you can sail in the opposite direction, if you want. That is a sure way to find rough water. But as you sail in the direction that your mothership wants to sail; your life fills with meaning, and purpose, and love."

Once we learn to surrender to the guidance of our souls, we can trust that we will always be guided towards our heart's desires and that which is aligned with our highest good. Our task is to ensure that our minds are not blocking the good with beliefs that do not serve. We must create conditions and an atmosphere in our minds that is conducive to the harmonics of the soul. The life you desire is already one with your soul, but it cannot manifest until you align with it and remove the blocks and hindrances of your mind. So, to begin, we must learn to shape our thoughts and beliefs in ways that serve.

Shaping Our Lives with Our Thoughts

We are programmed to think certain ways about every single aspect of our lives. Family, friends, money, work, health, sex, gender, school, grades, government, nations, community, etc. Sometimes, what we learn serves us. Oftentimes, it does not. Think about messages that you may have received and believed at a young age and how these messages shaped your life. Were you told you were smart? Were you around people who affirmed your beauty? Or, did you receive messages that caused you to question yourself? Whatever the case, you began to navigate life with a defined set of beliefs about yourself and the world. And what you may not realize is these beliefs, which are simply patterned ways of thinking, are directing your life. In essence, your thoughts are shaping your life experiences. Whatever you think about or focus on with consistency, you become. In this regard, your thoughts can support you with creating the life you desire, as illuminated by the guidance of your soul, or they can keep you stuck in fearful loops that consistently yield the same unwanted results. Many great philosophers and spiritual teachers have spoken about the power of our thoughts.

Siddhārtha Gautama, Buddha:
"All that we are is the result of what we have thought."

Chinese Philosopher, Lao Tzu:
"If you correct your mind, the rest of your life will fall into place."

Writer and Philosopher, Henry David Thoreau:
*"As a single footstep will not make a path on the earth,
so a single thought will not make a pathway in the mind.
To make a deep physical path, we walk again and again.
To make a deep mental path, we must think over and over
the kind of thoughts we wish to dominate our lives."*

Apostle Paul, from Philippians 4:8:
"Finally, brethren, whatsoever things are true, whatsoever things are honest, whatsoever things are just, whatsoever things are pure, whatsoever things are lovely, whatsoever things are of good report; if there be any virtue, and if there be any praise, think on these things."

When our thoughts are in alignment with the perspective of our souls, we consciously create lives that reflect our heart's desires. Conversely, when we leave our thoughts unchecked, they direct our lives in a way that feels like fate. Our beliefs and our thoughts are the tools that either open us to alignment or keep us disconnected and in our own way.

Our Thoughts Spark Our Emotions

Our thoughts will always generate an emotional response. Think a happy thought, and you feel happy. Think about something that terrifies you, and you feel frightened. We already noted that our thoughts either move us towards or away from our own alignment. Our emotions, then, are the magnificent indicators that let us know in which direction our thoughts are moving us. Again, either towards alignment or not. We will return to our emotions later, but for now, know that your emotions can be considered as your own personal GPS system, letting you know where you stand in relation to the perspective of your own soul. You should also know that the better you feel, the more in alignment you are with your soul. So, the goal is to think thoughts that bring you into alignment with the True You. Sounds simplistic, I know, but please read on.

The Benefits of Alignment

When you are in alignment, you are able to tune to the guidance of your own soul. This guidance feels different for each of us, but it often feels like an idea or impulse that lands on you. Go here. Do this. Call this person. Say this. This is what some call a state of flow, and it's the key to becoming a deliberate creator. When we're in flow (or alignment), we open to our capacity and power to create our lives by design, which is done by directing our thoughts and using our emotions to guide us. Another powerful benefit is this... when we are in alignment, we carry an energetic edge that amplifies our presence and powers our actions. Have you ever been around someone whose very presence alone felt powerful and life-giving? I assure you that people who vibe like this maintain a steady alignment.

Conversely, have you been around someone whose energy felt heavy, closed, or negative? In this case, you simply witnessed someone who was out of alignment with who they truly are. When someone is aligned, they radiate a power that connects with the best in others. Other people like to be around them. They feel lifted by them. They want to be of service to them because the truth of who they are is attracted to the truth that the aligned person is exuding.

These elements make life easier. When we are aligned, we experience more ease, grace, and flow. Instead of battling against life, we learn to yield and flow with the divine stream. How do we know when we are aligned? We know that we are aligned when we feel good. Our hearts are open. Our sense of faith feels grounded. We are optimistic about life. We see the good in others. We notice possibilities. We feel clear and connected to the present moment. We feel alive. We feel sure. We feel at peace. We feel safe. We know that we belong. And we feel worthy. When we are aligned, we notice how things are working in our favor. We struggle less and trust more, and our lives feel abundant and free. When we are aligned, our relationships feel easy, and we don't feel compelled to force people to show up the way that we "think" they should. When we are aligned, we don't fight against the circumstances of our lives. Rather, we trust that our well-being is assured. We know in our heart of hearts that it's all okay. The highest level of alignment is what we have come to know as unconditional love. No judgement. No demands. Total acceptance and allowance of all that is.

Our Thoughts and the Law of Attraction

There are many universal laws that govern our existence, but there is one that powerfully influences our capacity as creators. This law is commonly known as the Law of Attraction, and it is undergirded by the belief that our thoughts create. Whatever our thoughts are about ourselves and the world, the Universe will always respond with, "Yes, you are correct. Have more." In this sense, we get what we think about in that "like attracts like." Whatever we're emitting, in terms of our thoughts and emotions, the Universe will bring more of that to us. It's a way of ensuring that we always get to see who we are being and what we are choosing.

What we are emitting, at any given point, is known as our emotional "state of being" and largely determines what we attract into our lives. For example, when we're happy (state of being), it often seems that good things come our way. Conversely, when we're angry or mad (state of being), the reverse happens, and more things to be mad or angry about seem to come our way. Again, the Law of Attraction will always bring us more of what we're focused on and that which is in line with our state of being in any moment. In this way, our emotions serve as a gauge that lets us know where we are, where we are heading, and what we are calling to us.

Thanks to the work of researchers and scientists such as David Hawkins, author of "Power vs Force," we have been able to codify our emotions and better understand the information that they provide. Hawkins did research to map our emotions using a muscle testing technique called Applied Kinesiology. The science is based on the belief that various muscles are linked to certain organs and glands in the body. Accordingly, certain muscles will go weak when there is a pathology in an associated organ or gland. Over time, researchers concluded that muscle testing could also be used to determine what is good or bad for our bodies. Essentially, our bodies are connected to Universal consciousness, and as such, we can use them to determine if something is true or false. If something is true, the muscle stays strong. If it's false, it goes weak. Using this method, Hawkins developed a "scale of consciousness" that ranks our emotions. Here is a representation of that scale:

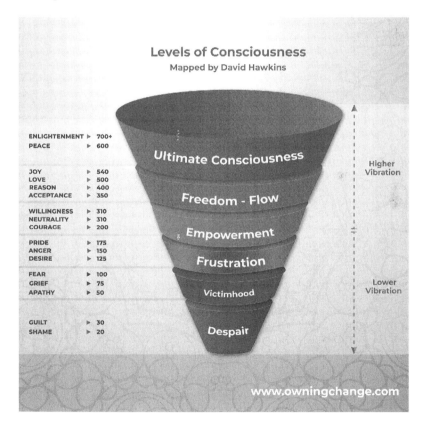

We all move through the range of these emotions at different times, but we tend to stabilize in a certain range. Hawkins believed that most of us dwell most consistently in the range of neutrality or around 250, in terms of our overall state of being, while masters such as Jesus and Buddha were thought to live at 1000, the level of enlightenment.

Everything in this world is made of energy, moving or "vibrating" at different rates or frequencies, and this includes our emotions. Negative emotions are dense vibrations and feel heavy and burdensome, whereas positive emotions feel light. When we vibrate along the lower range of emotions such as fear, grief, apathy, and shame, we lose our connection with our higher self. Said differently, we are no longer in alignment with our True Self or soul self. Conversely, when we land in the higher states of being, such as peace, love, and joy, we feel aligned or "at one" with who we truly are. Wherever we are, we can trust that the Law of Attraction will bring other thoughts and experiences that match our state of consciousness.

As you align with your True Self, you should use knowledge of the emotional scale to understand where you are and what's available to you. For example, if you are experiencing grief, anger is higher on the vibrational scale, so even a shift to that point is, ironically, moving towards love. This is why counselors and therapists will be pleased to see someone who's felt stuck in a place of despair gain enough energy and resolve to move into anger. Though anger is still a low-level vibration, it still feels better than grief, guilt, and shame.

It's difficult to jump from a lower-level vibration to a high one, so the goal is always to simply aim for a better feeling thought that will land us in a higher vibrational place, even if only slightly higher. Then, from there, we can continue to choose thoughts that move us higher and higher on the scale.

As you see from the scale, pride, anger, desire (craving, addiction & lust), fear, apathy, grief, guilt, and shame are low-level vibrations and land us in the space of despair, victimhood, and frustration. At these levels, we feel powerless. By contrast, once we land at the level of courage, we begin to reclaim our power on our way towards higher vibrations such as acceptance, reason, love, and joy.

The Law of Attraction and Spiritual Bypassing

The Law of Attraction has been the focal point of lots of debates, many centered around criticism that the law encourages what some call "spiritual bypassing." This means that in an attempt to stay in a high vibe state, some will either (1) suppress negative emotions and deny what they are truly feeling or (2) ignore the real problems of their lives and this world by sticking their heads in the sand. Both things are possible and can lead to negative consequences; therefore, they are worthy of our consideration.

Let's first discuss negative emotions. Emotions are felt in the body, and they are meant to move by definition. When we learn to observe them and not get entangled with them, i.e., allowing them to pass through our bodies, then we are able to use them as information. The challenge arises when we fearfully identify with the emotion and disallow it. By the time we feel any emotion, the thought that has generated it has done its work. At that point, the goal is to feel what we feel and to decide where we want to go from there. If we continue to feed our minds the same thoughts that created the feeling, the emotion will likely persist or worsen. Also, if we identify with the feeling, e.g., "I am angry" vs. "I feel angry," then we are giving the emotion more power and authority than necessary.

The goal of acknowledging the Law of Attraction is not to attempt to close ourselves off to a world where we only feel positive emotions. Rather, it's to understand that our emotions are there to offer us useful information about where we are on our journeys and to course correct, IF necessary and IF we choose to. Sometimes, I will dip into a negative emotion, and I will not have the desire or will to immediately shift out of it. During these times, I will allow the feeling to linger until I'm ready to get back on track and back into alignment. But I try to remain as the conscious observer, maintaining some space between my awareness and the emotion, lest I become lost in what I'm feeling. Also, the more I use my spiritual tools, the more stable I become in staying in a high vibe space. So, now, when I dip into negative emotions, I usually cannot tolerate it for too long because I don't like the feeling of being out of alignment. It feels like my soul is in one room and I'm in another, and the distance feels too uncomfortable to withstand for too long.

So, please move forward knowing that part of the beauty of the human experience is our capacity to experience the full range of our emotions. And even if you choose to aim for living in a high vibe space as much as you can, this does not mean that you should not acknowledge or suppress negative emotions. Rather, you should use all of your emotions as information about where your personality stands in relation to your soul.

The second concern about "sticking your head in the ground" and ignoring problems is a bit more complex. Thoughts create, and what you focus on expands. Have you ever been in a situation where you bought something, for example, a red car, and afterwards you seemed to notice your red car everywhere? What happened? Did everyone go out and buy a red car at the same time? Of course not. What happened is red cars were at the forefront of your mind, and so you noticed them more. The same holds true for everything; whatever you give your attention to expands in your awareness. If you walk around thinking most people are angry and nuts, then those are the people you will find on your path. This is conscious creation. It's what you're giving your attention to, and the Law of Attraction does its work by bringing you more of the same.

For this reason, we do want to be sure that we are not fixated on the problems of our lives and this world because when we are, we grow them with our thoughts and awareness. We are better served when we acknowledge the challenge and then direct our thoughts towards what we want to create versus what we don't want. For example, if we focus on ridding the world of war, our thoughts are still on war, which creates more of it. Conversely, if we focus on peace, that expands, and it sends our energy and efforts in a different direction. It's commonly held that this explains the reason why so many campaigns, such as the "War Against Drugs" or the "War Against Poverty," perpetuate the very problems we are attempting to dismantle. In her wisdom, Mother Teresa is famously known for saying, "I was once asked why I don't participate in anti-war demonstrations. I said that I will never do that, but as soon as you have a pro-peace rally, I'll be there."

This is why I firmly believe we have made minimal progress in our attempt to root out many of the isms of the world because we are constantly focused on the pain of what is versus what we want to be. Instead of focusing on the vision of a more beautiful world, we are fixated on the problems and the brokenness. We know what's wrong. We don't need to continue to illuminate our challenges. We must figure out a way to amplify the vision of what's possible. In this vein, Albert Einstein noted, "No problem can be solved from the same level of consciousness that created it."

We are all subject to the Law of Attraction, whether we realize it or not. And if we misunderstand or abuse the law, it doesn't make the law any less potent or real. We are all co-creators of our own reality. Most, however, create lives by default, not understanding their power or capacity to influence their own lives. By understanding and utilizing the Law of Attraction, you will become a deliberate creator, using your thoughts to contour your life and your emotions as your powerful guide.

A Major Shift for a Client

I have personally experienced phenomenal changes in my life by applying these laws and principles, but instead of sharing one of my own stories, I'd actually like to share (with permission) the story of one of my beloved clients, who I will call Marissa. Marissa came to me because she was frustrated in her current position and she wanted to find a new job. She had enjoyed a good measure of success with her company, but she was challenged, particularly by her boss. She felt that he constantly overlooked her and ignored her contributions, though they were stellar.

I always explain to my clients that I never work to just assist my clients with finding another job. We eventually get to the practical work of detailing resumes and fine-tuning job search strategies, but it's not where we start. We start with working to get an understanding of what's unfolding spiritually. Because we create our own reality, if we're stuck in a situation that's painful, then we can change jobs and even move to another city, but the situation will meet us there. This is why we see so many reliving the same painful situations over and over again.

So, with Marissa. We did the soul work first. I taught her the details of the principles I'm sharing with you, and she trusted the process enough to consider how she'd been inviting the same results based on her beliefs and expectations. Her supervisor was repeatedly giving her the same response because that's what she was focused on and thereby strengthening. When she was convinced that she had the power to create a new narrative, she did! By shifting her thoughts and choosing to focus on what she wanted versus what she didn't want, her situation completely changed. A few months after our coaching had ended, Marissa shared her incredible success story with me about how her supervisor had started to go above and beyond in recognizing her efforts. Also, not only had their relationship changed, but the dynamic and interactions with her entire team had also changed.

One of the things that Marissa learned was how she had been closed off in how she was showing up to work. Like many, she'd come to believe that being professional meant leaving parts of herself at the door. As we unlocked key soul qualities like authenticity and vulnerability, she started to show up differently. She happily reported that she felt freer and more open at work and, for the first time, was happily engaging with her team. She was more open and playful and gave herself permission to be free.

Marissa's story has always been special to me because there was such a dramatic opening in her world. And as you can probably imagine, these tools don't just unlock one part of your life, they unlock your life, all of it. In our periodic check-ins, Marissa continues to demonstrate just what a powerful creator she is. So, my recommendation to you is to give it a try. Sit with the information I've shared and try it on to see what shifts you might create in your own life. The power tools shared on the following pages will support you in unlocking your own life and stepping into your divine right place as a powerful creator.

The Hard Parts

Alignment is not something you achieve once and then you're done. Like much of life, we witness ebbs and flows and times when we feel stable in our alignment, as well as times when we question everything we once thought we knew. If you consider the mothership analogy offered by Gary Zukav, as he noted, the mothership knows everything about our lives, i.e., why we're where we are in the water, why we may be encountering a storm, etc. We, on the other hand, are unable to see things from the highest perspective, and this can cause us to sometimes struggle and doubt. It's why we must, by faith, commit to following the mothership in the first place.

I know the sweetness of alignment, and I have tremendous gratitude when I'm in that space. And I'm also thankful that, by grace, I am able to maintain a steady sense of alignment most of the time. With that, however, in addition to my own moments of frustration and doubt, I acknowledge that our journeys are all different, with varying degrees of difficulties and challenges to overcome. The picture that I paint of what's possible is offered with tremendous humility. It's not easy. And I do not share these ideas as a 1,2,3 step solution to the challenges you may be facing. Based on my studies of ancient wisdom, spirituality, and most importantly, my own lived experiences, I simply believe that it's "a" path, of many, that can lead us to higher ground.

As you journey on your own path, it is so super important that you envelop your entire being with as much love, gentleness, and tenderness as you possibly can. It's so easy for our spiritual journeys to become one more area of our lives layered by judgment and feelings of inadequacy. If that happens for you at any point (and it will), know that wherever you are, it is all okay. As my friend and former coach, Lisa Berkovitz says, "Let it be easy." You are fundamentally beautiful, magnificent, and divine, and there's nothing you can ever do that will change the truth of who you are. Rest in that.

My final word of caution is this. I honestly believe that we choose to come to the planet for different experiences and different reasons. When we look at the intense suffering of many in this world, it can be difficult to embrace much of what I'm sharing about our being creators of our own realities. Why would anyone choose suffering? For most of us, the point is, it's not something that we are consciously choosing. We suffer because we have not discovered our power to shape our experiences. Simultaneously, I believe that there are innocent souls who are born with the express purpose of opening the rest of us to unconditional love. Our divine essence is eternal. The soul of who we are existed before we incarnated and will exist after we leave this earthly plane. And we can never know the purpose and mission of another soul.

We don't fully understand all of the details of this existence. It's why we walk by faith. My encouragement to you is to take the parts of this book that resonate with you and try them on. Take the tools that I'm offering and see if they positively impact your life. Ultimately, I believe they have the capacity to lead us all towards a world where we can know the felt experience of love.

Align Power Tools

Power of Thoughts

"If you are distressed by anything external, the pain is not due to the thing itself, but to your estimate of it; and this you have the power to revoke at any moment."
—Marcus Aurelius

Here are some tools you can use to begin to cultivate thoughts that move you towards alignment.

Soothe Yourself

Soothing is based on the belief that in all things, the Universe is conspiring on our behalf. Things are always working in our favor. Even when it may appear otherwise. This is the core essence of faith. The Mind of God is greater than anything we can fully comprehend, and so our job is to trust that things are working in our favor, even when it doesn't feel like it. With soothing, we talk to ourselves lovingly and remind ourselves that everything is okay and just as it's supposed to be. Find general words and phrases that soothe you. My go-to is,

"All is well." As you begin to think in this way, you will start to see evidence of its truth. I think of these types of phrases as anchors, and I use them all day, every day. Another favorite is, "Things are always working out for me," which I use whenever my thoughts turn to worry. It immediately reminds me to shift back to the present moment. These phrases have become second nature to me and evoke an immediate feeling of groundedness and peace.

Reframe

When we have an initial negative response to a situation, we can attempt to shift how we are viewing it and aim to see it from the perspective of our soul, which recognizes the beauty and value in all things. This is the equivalent of "finding the good." Ask powerful questions, such as *"What's good about this?" "What's the gift in this?"* and *"How is this serving me?"* Powerful questions yield powerful answers and move you into alignment. Disempowering questions take you out of alignment. Reframing is significantly connected to the belief that those things that we place our attention on, grow in our experience and awareness. So, you want to put your mind to work on an aspect of the situation that serves you.

Affirm

Mantras and affirmations are powerful. As we've noted, you are always creating. And you've been using affirmations, by default, to create. Think about the negative messages you've been telling yourself over and over? Now it's time to replace those with new ones that move you towards alignment. The key to affirmations is affirming things that feel at least a bit resonant. From there, you then work your way towards more specific ones. For example, if you feel completely unstable financially, then affirming, *"I am a millionaire"* will not move your forward. It's probably too far out of reach to evoke an emotional connection. However, a more general statement such as, *"I am divinely cared for, and I have everything that I need"* may carry just enough resonant truth to make you believe in that direction. And then, as the truth of this statement settles in, you can begin to build on it. Also, remember to affirm in the present tense as if it's already true or done. This is a powerful tool of creation. Speak God's promises over your life. Not as a reminder to God but as a way of tuning yourself to the good that is already yours.

Look for What You Want to See

Because we create with our attention and focus, one of the most powerful things you can do to intentionally create and manifest your desires is put your attention on those things in your life that you want to grow. Notice what's right in your life and notice what's right in the world.

Set Intentions

Create a container for your day and for experiences that you want to influence. At the start of the day, speak your intention out loud or silently. An example is, *"May I meet every moment with a spirit of peace."* You can also use intentions when walking into situations that you want to shape. Perhaps it's an important conversation or an important meeting. Your intention, in either case, might be something like, *"I will move through this with ease, compassion, and grace."*

Surround Yourself with Positive Messages

Flood your favorite spot at home or your office with messages that remind you of who you are. This is aimed at reprogramming the default thinking that's been running the show thus far. Go back to the section on "soothing" and translate those types of messages into written form.

Watch for Energy Leaks

Watch for the thoughts that take you out of alignment. Judgment, i.e., "the shoulds and the shouldn'ts" are at the top of the list. One key to being a powerful creator is allowing what is to be. There's no need to push against anything... circumstances... decisions made... other people's views of who they think you are. It's all okay. Everyone's trying to find their way back home... to their True Self, and there's this stuff that's happening along the way. It's all okay. Accordingly, we get to release judgments about it. Spiritual teacher Carolyn Myss says, "There is no right or wrong and heaven does not punish." Rumi said, "Out beyond ideas of wrongdoing and right doing there is a field. I'll meet you there." Other energy leaks include comparisons, lack of forgiveness, regret over the past, and anxiety about the future. When you find yourself in negative loops and "leaking" related to any of these things, your only job is to shift your attention towards something that feels better. You don't have to try to dig up the past and fix it.

Align Reflective Questions

1. *How would you describe the dominant voice that occupies your thoughts? Is it positive or negative? How did this voice come to be? Who and what influenced it?*

2. *Are your thoughts predominantly about the past, present, or future?*

3. *What stories do you tell yourself about yourself and your life? Do these stories help or hinder you?*

4. *When you observe your thoughts, who or what is doing the observing?*

5. *How have your beliefs shaped you? Do all of your beliefs belong to you?*

6. *How would you describe the lens through which you see the world? Are you more inclined to notice what's right or what's wrong?*

7. *How do you view your purpose? Do you feel connected to it?*

Align Soul Quality

Responsibility

*"Taking 100 percent responsibility for your life is the path
of spiritual growth, of total freedom. Being a spirit having a
human experience means we have to step fully into life. Into our
roles, actions and emotions. When have you felt like a victim or
decided to take responsibility? Think back through your past.
How can you begin to own every aspect of your life?"*
— SHAKTI SUTRIASA

Aligning helps to unlock your sense of responsibility by bringing awareness to how you think and respond to life. As you build this muscle, you will learn to take ownership and accountability for your experiences. Every action, thought, choice, or deed is a vote for what you want to see more of in the world.

One of the most pronounced ways that responsibility plays out is in how you feel. We have been trained to lay blame on others for how we feel, putting an unfair burden and responsibility on another for our own emotional landscape. When we allow another person's actions to dictate how we feel, then we are relinquishing our power.

No one can make you angry. No one can make you sad. No one can make you feel anything. Whatever you feel is the result of a thought that you are choosing. It's the result of the perspective that you are holding about the person or the situation. Your feelings can change at any moment, with the choice to shift your perspective. I know, this feels a bit tricky, right? Does this mean that others are absolved of any responsibility for their behavior? What it means is their choices and their path are theirs and yours are yours. Because we are communal beings, we can express our desires, and we can even establish boundaries, but ultimately, we would not want anyone else to carry the responsibility of determining *our* peace, joy, and happiness because we are then at the mercy of their choices.

Furthermore, we must understand that anything that triggers a negative emotion in us is an invitation to look within, not to try to fix the stimulus out there. If someone hurts your feelings in some way, that hurt is pointing to a wound that is offering itself up to be healed. It's your responsibility to examine the part of you that resonated with the offense. If someone calls me an idiot, their words cannot touch me unless there's a part of me, no matter how small, that questions or agrees with what they said. When we become defensive and hurt by anything, there is a hint of resonance somewhere. So, we learn not to waste energy on the offender. Rather, we have a talk with our own soul in an attempt to understand where the original wound lies.

Similarly, when we are challenged by life circumstances, we have a choice about how we respond. You get to choose a perspective that serves you or one that hinders you. You get to ask empowering questions that open you to peace. Or you can ask disempowering questions that make you feel like a victim. There's no judgment in your choice, and sometimes the weight of life can land us in a place that's so painful that it doesn't even feel like we have a choice. But the reality is we can always invite grace to illuminate our minds and open our awareness to the power that we have within.

Responsibility plays out in other ways as well. In addition to owning your feelings and response to what happens to you, you get to consciously create the atmosphere around you based on your patterned thoughts. You can own your choice to beautify the world with your talents and gifts and to walk deliberately in your purpose. You can own your choice to be true to yourself and follow your own path. You can own the change that you want to see in your life. You can own the change you want to see in the world by becoming what you want to see more of, and you can own that whatever you're being adds to the collective atmosphere.

PART III:
FLOW

Let it Go and Let it Flow

"Those who flow as life flows know they need no other force."
– Lao Tzu

My family and I experienced so much grace during those "desert years." So many lessons. So much unfolding. So much growth. We flailed around for a while with the initial attempt to do the work we'd set out to do. As far as know-how, I was not completely new to entrepreneurship since I'd owned the spa party business, though I'd soon learn that selling spa parties and selling myself were two totally different animals. And as for my husband, all of it was completely new territory for him. His efforts lasted for a few months, and soon thereafter, he accepted the reality that we needed to generate income, and he did what he had to do. He eventually returned to the classroom with brief stints and forays into other jobs, some of which were painful for him to endure. For my part, I took on an interim post that lasted a few months but primarily focused on trying to make my business work, which my husband patiently supported.

That was the summary. These are the details. This time was challenging, consuming, humiliating, and confusing, and it left us wide open and vulnerable in many ways. There were many days when we carried guilt about our choices and days when we sat in fear of not knowing how we would ever rebound. We had a mortgage, debt, and a family to take care of, and at times, the weight of these things felt unbearable. Simultaneously, however, there was another narrative springing forth that was equally powerful and true. Amid managing the bumps and bruises, when we paid attention, we realized that somehow, things always worked out.

I could write multiple chapters on the grace-fueled events and situations that ended with us being the recipient of many beautiful, unanticipated gifts. The emotional suffering that we experienced was largely self-imposed, for somehow so much goodness still found its way to our door despite where we stood financially. Our home was saved, vacations were gifted to us, my daughter was able to complete a degree at an Ivy League institution, and so much more. Resources appeared out of nowhere. One of my favorites was a perfectly timed letter that I received about money in a retirement account that I knew nothing about that had to be withdrawn. Another favorite was a hailstorm that came through that did just enough damage to our cedar roof that it allowed us to receive close to $40,000 in home repairs. Prior to the storm, the roof was at the point where it needed to be replaced, and the interior of our home needed to be painted as well. But given the situation we were in, neither of these things was a priority. The storm brought with it a new roof and a paint job for a room where it caused a leak. The additional wink from God came when we realized that due to our home's open floor plan, the contractors had to paint, not just the one room, but the entire downstairs because there was no natural break between rooms.

Looking back, I can see where the Universe was whispering at every turn, "Surrender. Let go. I've got this." But oftentimes, it was only in retrospect that we saw and acknowledged God's handiwork.

And we'd question, on the backend, why we were so reluctant to release the worry and doubt. Over time, my faith muscles did grow, but it wasn't until another magnificent moment of grace that the theme of surrender would land on me so mightily that it would render its power undeniable.

At the top of 2018, I made what felt like a last-ditch effort to breathe life into my business. I'd had varying degrees of success with obtaining both private and corporate clients. Still, I had not found my way towards creating reliable systems and structures to generate predictable, sustainable income. As I mentioned, my husband had been extremely patient with me as I tried to make things work, but he was growing weary, and I knew that I needed to consistently relieve some of the financial pressure. So, in January of that year, I offered a free week-long program for women with the intention of having it serve as a feeder into an extended paid group coaching program. I was so excited about the offer because I knew that it would be powerful. And if it worked, all I would need to do was wash, rinse, and repeat. I enrolled more than 200 women into the feeder program, and based on my goals, I knew that I only needed about 5-10% of those participants to say "Yes" to my paid program. So, I ran the program, received phenomenal feedback, opened the doors to the paid program, and it completely and utterly flopped. Someone, please pass the job ads.

I reluctantly commenced with looking for a job. By this time, I had substantial experience with coaching and training, and though I was extremely resistant, I was confident that I could land a role. I knew that I needed to do what I needed to do, but once again, I was so confused. I knew how to listen and follow the guidance of my soul, and the messaging I'd received was about being positioned for the next level. My breakthrough felt imminent. A few months before, I'd created a vision board that I called the "Career and Finance" edition, and I felt so much resonance with all of the good that I'd detailed on that board. I just knew it would come to pass, and I believed that my business would be the vehicle. So, when reality set in that I needed to put my business down and find a job, I was completely confused.

I had a few interviews and ultimately landed an offer as a Learning & Development Specialist with a local governmental agency. The Hail Mary I hoped for in my business did not come. I was distraught. So much so that I took the vision board I'd created, and I put it in the trash. I was dumbfounded and angry with the Universe... once again.

I remember retreating to my bathtub, as is customary, to work things out. As soon as I sat in the tub, the floodgates opened. I sobbed and sobbed... and sobbed some more. Total ugly cry. I let it all out, and I purged. And then... I lifted my head and surrendered. By the time I got out, I was ready to move forward. I'd decided that if I had to take the job, the organization would not receive part of me or a diminished me. They would receive all of me. I'd go in fully present, ready to offer myself in the best and highest way.

If someone had told me that I would find peace and happiness in any 9-5 role, let alone a role with the government, I would have kindly declared them insane. And yet I stand before you to report that the job was perfect. My supervisor, my team, the organization, the environment, the people and the work, the autonomy, all perfect. The only challenge was my commute, and even that, the Universe miraculously resolved. At one point, I had an intuitive consultation with a healer friend who told me that somehow my commute would be made lovely. Once the 2020 pandemic hit, everything shifted, and with more people working remotely, traffic became a non-issue. Once again, in a way that I could have never imagined, the Universe delivered.

About eight months or so into the position, I decided to do a class on visioning, and as I was preparing, I thought about the vision board that I had created and trashed. As I was thinking, I remembered that, for whatever reason, I'd taken a picture of the vision board. So, I searched my phone, scrolling through numerous pictures, until I found it. When I saw it, I was floored. No less than 75-80% of what

I'd detailed on that board had come to pass. I'd envisioned myself in front of more people. The new role brought with it responsibility for the learning and development of more than 5000 employees. I'd wanted to take my work international. A few months earlier, I'd been contracted to do some work in Turks and Caicos with an opportunity that landed out of the blue. I'd wanted to expand my wardrobe. Check. I wanted a new car. We got not one new car, but two. On and on, the vision had come to pass. There was just one minor detail with how it all played out. When I created the board, I fully expected my business to be the sole vehicle for delivering the goods, but the Universe obviously had a different plan.

There was so much for me to gain from this unexpected path. It was a new, creative space for me to grow my skills and my confidence. I gained the financial stability that allowed me and my family to breathe. And since I no longer "needed" my business to work, I was able to play and enjoy it on a part-time basis in new ways. So many gifts.

From this experience, I learned three things. First, I learned the incredible, life-giving power of surrender. Second, I learned that the Universe is constantly working to deliver the desires of our hearts. And third, I learned that we must detach and release all expectations of how the good is packaged and delivered. It truly was the space of this experience that moved me from head knowing to heart knowing. Now, I doubt less and trust a whole lot more.

The Role of Surrender as We Unfold

"If you surrender to the wind, you can ride it."
– Toni Morrison

When we spoke about alignment, I explained that the goal is to tune into and follow the guidance of our souls, which are aligned with the mind of God. To do so, we need to release the reigns and fully trust. Surrender carries with it a feeling of lightness and release. We're no longer clinging and trying to force a particular outcome. We allow. In surrender, we trust that there is a greater wisdom that exists that's far beyond anything that we can concoct with our own minds. Accordingly, we let go, and we trust that whatever unfolds is for our best and highest good. This can be extremely challenging at times because the ego, which always seeks certainty, loves to control. It wants to be in charge. For the ego, "Thy will be done" is foreign and scary territory.

But the rewards of surrender are plentiful. When we surrender, we feel boundless, peaceful, and fearless, and instead of working against it, we are able to flow with life. Author Debbie Ford explained, "Surrender is a gift that you can give yourself. It's an act of faith. It's saying that even though I can't see where this river is flowing, I trust it will take me in the right direction." The way that I can feel into whether or not I've surrendered is by tuning to whether my thoughts feel upstream or downstream, a way of looking at things that I derived from spiritual teacher Esther Hicks. If I feel like I'm grappling and trying to force a solution, that feels upstream. Conversely, the space of surrender and letting go feels downstream.

It's also important to understand that a lack of surrender puts us in the way of the breakthrough. It's as if God can't manage the work to be done if we're busy fiddling with it. I'm sure you've heard stories where someone received the breakthrough at the moment that they surrendered. I've always appreciated the story shared by Oprah Winfrey about her big moment of surrender. She explained that she was obsessed with the book "The Color Purple" and, through happenstance, was afforded an opportunity to audition for a role in the movie. After auditioning, Oprah explained that after a while, she was in fits because she hadn't heard about final decisions. One day, while out walking, she found herself completely stressing about the part, when in a moment of grace, she decided to surrender. The tears flowed, and she let it go. In that exact moment, she said that someone came out to her to say that she had a phone call. It was Steven Spielberg. She got the part.

A lack of surrender lands us in a space of worry, and worry is a low vibe space that hinders our alignment. And because like attracts like, worry begets worry. Whatever the challenge, offer it to the divine as often as necessary. Sometimes we have to release the same issue over and over again. Let it go. Imagine it in your mind's eye and see yourself offering it to God or letting it go in some other way. For example, my sister gifted me with a visualization that I find very powerful, and I use it often, especially when I'm concerned about an issue with my daughters. I imagine the divine as a bright force sitting in the middle of a prism of light. I take my daughters by the hand, walk into the prism, put their hands in the hand of the divine, and I walk away. You can also use techniques like writing a letter and burning it or journaling and simply writing about what you are ready to release.

Lightening Our Loads

"Humbleness, forgiveness, clarity and love are the dynamics of freedom. They are the foundations of authentic power."
– GARY ZUKAV

"Flow." I love the word. It engenders a vision of lightness and ease. In surrender, we flow when we let go, allowing the current to carry us wherever it chooses, trusting that it will always land us in a place of beauty. But even in our deliberateness to surrender the direction of our lives, our journeys are burdened if we are carrying an undue load. Imagine someone traveling through the airport. Even if they humbly follow the signs and the guidance of helpful employees along the way, their trip will feel hampered if they are traveling with heavy baggage.

We learned in Part II, Align, that the goal is to manage our minds, so we see things through the eyes of our soul. It's what some refer to as wearing our "god-glasses," i.e., seeing things from a higher perspective. We trust that things are somehow always working in our favor. No resistance. In this way, we don't pick up the weights of life, to begin with. However, in our humanity, at times, our god-glasses may be outside of our reach, and we will struggle as we navigate loss, disappointments, relationship woes, injustice, traumatic events, and more. When this happens, we are reminded to do the work of acknowledging and allowing the associated feelings that rise, lathering them with love, and sitting with them as long as necessary. And then, by grace, we choose to let the grievance or injury go. Oftentimes, this type of release is the energetic partner of surrender known as "forgiveness," where we are called to forgive either ourselves, others, or Life.

Forgiving Ourselves

I grew up in a conservative Christian household where my initial spiritual formation was rooted in the belief that we are sinful by nature. And though I have come to understand Jesus and his teachings in a new way, my foundation as a child was about learning to censor my "impure" self. My family still teases me about the time when a well-meaning relative spied me out at the school sock hop and provided a full report to my parents about my sinful dancing. Things that were a natural part of the landscape of a child's life were met with doctrine, rules, and dogma that caused me to question myself at every turn. By the time I was an adult, I was a master at judging myself.

Where religion left off, other forms of cultural and societal programming came in to solidify my self-judgment. Was I helpful enough? Caring enough? Brave enough? Loving enough? Pure enough? Why did I say that? Why did I do that? Why did I believe that? Why did I choose that? The constant condemnation that we endure can, at times, be all-consuming as we declare ourselves wrong in so many ways. And though the antidote to the judgment feels like forgiveness, in truth, there is nothing to forgive.

We all make decisions and choices based on our level of consciousness at any given moment. Even if someone commits a horrible act or injustice against another, it's because, in that moment, they were disconnected from the truth of who they really are. This is represented in the magnitude of the words offered by Jesus when, upon being crucified, he prayed, "Father, forgive them for they know not what they do." And even in this exhortation, it is more accurate to see Jesus' words as a declaration rather than an appeal because in the eyes of God, no one is ever condemned. There is nothing to forgive.

Similarly, know that any judgment that you direct towards yourself is the result of the false accusations of your ego or small self. The True You, your soul self, never condemns. It only holds you in the light of what it knows you to truly be, which is a direct extension of God. The True You never blames or shames. It stands firm in its knowing that you are worthy, loving you unconditionally and without rebuke.

In this sense, we can view forgiveness as letting go of false beliefs and returning to the truth of who we really are. Incidentally, this understanding was brought full circle for me upon discovering an enlightened perspective on the meaning of sin. The metaphysical definition translates sin as "missing the mark" and explains that it is associated with "wrong thinking." In essence, it's a state of consciousness or belief that we are alienated or separate from God. In this state, we make choices based on lack and fear. To correct this then, we move towards "right thinking" by remembering who we are.

This releasing and remembering... this "forgiving" ... removes the weights that impact our alignment and hinder our flow. Remember that emotional scale? You are more buoyant and capable of landing in high vibe states when you are energetically clutter-free. And in this space, you can more easily tune to and hear the voice of your soul as it guides you on your path... unencumbered by unnecessary judgments against yourself.

Forgiving of Others

In a blog post that I wrote called "God Waits for Us," I share a story about Buck Brannaman, the leading horse trainer known as the

"Horse Whisperer." In the documentary about his life, there was a moment when Buck made the decision to euthanize a horse that he deemed dangerous and irredeemable. The horse had been deprived of oxygen during a difficult birth and landed in the hands of owners who neglected him. Eventually, he was delivered to new owners who, upon hearing about Buck's successes, made one final attempt at redemption. Buck agreed to see if the horse could be rehabilitated, but while on site, the horse attacked one of his assistants. From there, they decided that it had to be put down.

During a scene that gushed with compassion and grace, Buck patiently waited for the reluctant and unpredictable horse to make its way up the ramp and onto a trailer to be carried away, insisting that they not take him by force. As the horse bucked and stalled, he simply lowered his head and said, "We will wait." The onlookers, stunned by his restraint towards this dangerous horse that had harmed his assistant, later asked him why he chose to be so patient. Buck then explained, "I would never think to have contempt for the horse . . . he is simply the product of what he's been through."

The same rules that we discussed relative to self-forgiveness apply to others as well. Again, we all make choices based on our state of consciousness at any given moment. And we are all simply the products of what we've been through. The Universe knows this; therefore, there is never any condemnation. Just love. We can never know the depths of someone else's pain, and we can never know where they are on their soul journey. It's not for us to know. What we do know is that the same grace that we extend in releasing ourselves of judgment must be extended to others as well. "Father, forgive them, for they know not what they do." There's no judgment and no denunciation, and when we are at our best, our only wish is that they would be restored to their own "right thinking."

I know that this is a super "ginormous" pill to swallow, and yet this is the path of true awakening. This is the path towards unconditional love. This is the path of remembering who we are. The veil is lifted, and we discover that the harm that we may have endured at the hand of another was the result of their own fear-based, wrongful thinking. Another way of framing this is by looking at a quote from the book, "A Course in Miracles," which says, "Everything is either an act of love or a call for love." Any hurt directed towards us is a call for love.

Viewing forgiveness of others this way is something that we must work towards, and just like everything else, our muscles are strengthened by spiritual practice. The goal, as we journey, is to be forgiving and patient with ourselves along the way as we learn to be patient and forgiving of others. Sometimes, the offense can be so piercing that it can take years for someone to forgive. My dear friend, Christy Sims, a well-known survivor and advocate against domestic violence, was disfigured at the hand of her ex-boyfriend, who doused her with sulfuric acid. Christy is one of the most authentic and beautiful souls imaginable, and I watched from the sidelines as she worked her way towards forgiveness of her attacker. What I loved so much about her example was how she owned every stage that she landed in and loved herself through the process of forgiveness, allowing as much time as she needed over a span of several years. True forgiveness cannot be feigned, and, in some cases, the grievance is so horrific that we must call on the force of grace itself to work our way towards release.

Another example of heroic forgiveness comes from Mary Johnson, whose story was featured on NPR's StoryCorps in 2011. Johnson's 20-year-old son, Laramiun Byrd, was killed by a 16-year-old boy by the name of Oshea Israel. Wanting to understand the mind of the person who took her son's life, Johnson made repeated requests to visit Israel in prison, and after several years, he acquiesced. Upon meeting and sharing, human to human, Johnson forgave Israel, even hugging him before she left. In the StoryCorps interview, Johnson speaks of that moment, saying to Israel, "And I instantly knew that all that anger and the animosity, all the stuff I had in my heart for

12 years for you — I knew it was over, that I had totally forgiven you." As of the release of that story, Israel had been discharged from prison, and the two enjoyed a close relationship as next-door neighbors.

Sometimes we're just as challenged by the petty grievances as we are by the obscene ones. Think of relationships where siblings don't speak for years over simple misunderstandings. Or friendships that fall apart for similar reasons. From working with employees, I have seen so many instances where a lack of forgiveness over the simplest of things wreaked havoc on performance and teams. Regardless of the magnitude of the perceived injustice, it can be extremely difficult, at times, to let go. And this unforgiveness does not come without cost. As I alluded earlier, the weight of these types of negative entanglements can keep us out of alignment with our true selves and, due to the energetic resistance, inhibit our sense of flow. In this regard, the choice to forgive can also be viewed as an act of self-care and self-love as resentment primarily hurts the one who carries it. After being released from an unjust prison sentence of 27 years, South African statesman Nelson Mandela said, "As I walked out the door toward the gate that would lead to my freedom, I knew if I didn't leave my bitterness and hatred behind, I'd still be in prison." Self-care. Self-love. All resentments can be remedied with a shift towards right thinking. And we can proceed by choosing love, establishing healthy boundaries, and allowing others to find their way.

Forgiving Life Itself

Life Coach Martha Beck often talks about the many gifts that came from having a son with Down syndrome. I once heard her say that whenever she meets women who tell her that they have given birth to a child with this condition, it takes everything within her to not yell, "Congratulations!" Based on her own experiences, she knows that they are in for a beautiful, heart-opening adventure. As I mentioned before, I see brave souls like Martha Beck's son, Adam, as coming to the planet for the express purpose of opening our hearts to unconditional love. They are those whose inner beauty demands that we see and embrace their differences. My nephew Aaryn stands boldly among them. Born with cerebral palsy and developmental delays, at age 18, he's never been able to walk or do anything independently. That withstanding, he is brilliantly gifted in his own way and helps us to see the purpose and value in every life. Aaryn has had several surgeries to correct various issues, and the pain he has endured has caused equal pain for his mom. And in situations like this, we often find ourselves saying, "But Universe, why?"

Whether it's witnessing the suffering of those we love or managing any of a host of other life challenges, sometimes we simply get mad at Life itself. Even from my place of privilege, I cannot tell you how many times I stopped speaking to Life because the two of us were just not on good terms. So, when those who truly suffer find it difficult to forgive, I totally and completely get it.

For my part, all that I know to do is return to my belief that even with the most unimaginable difficulties, our experiences are always purposeful and used in the service of our individual and collective awakening. In May of 2020, the whole world stood in horror at the death of African American George Floyd when a police officer kneeled on his neck for more than eight minutes, killing him. His crime? A store clerk alleged that he passed a false $20 bill. His death ignited a revolution and pierced the hearts of many who lived unaware of the challenges faced by people of color and the disproportionate use of force often used against them. Protests erupted around the world in a powerful show of solidarity by people who demanded that better must come. I was struck when I read that Floyd's young daughter had said to her mom, upon seeing widespread demonstrations, that "Daddy changed the world." Yes, sweetheart, he did.

In my heart of hearts, I believe that prior to incarnating, our souls collude with other souls and with the Universe as we detail our missions. And though I believe that sometimes sensitive souls may even have a conscious awareness of the painful roles they are to play, perhaps as in the case of Jesus, the greater part of me believes that their awareness is cushioned by grace. Clearly, some things we are meant to know and some things we must accept by faith. This faith is grounded in the understanding that the ways of the Universe exceed our capacity to understand what is fully at play. Einstein once said that the most important decision we could ever make is deciding whether we lived in a friendly or unfriendly Universe. If you believe that the Universe is inherently a benevolent force, then that means that "everything serves." Even the painful, unimaginable things that we may never fully understand... they serve.

Just as we are asked to release the judgments against ourselves and others, ultimately, we must offer the same of the Life and the Universe itself and trust in its divine plan. As Romans 8:28 declares, "And we know that all things work together for good to them that love God, to them who are called according to his purpose." This would include every one of us.

Shifting From Grit to Grace

*"When I run after what I think I want, my days are a
furnace of stress and anxiety; if I sit in my own place of
patience, what I need flows to me, and without pain. From
this I understand that what I want also wants me, is looking
for me and attracting me. There is a great secret here for
anyone who can grasp it."*

– RUMI

There is a lot of conversation in spiritual circles about manifestation, which is using spiritual principles and tools to bring one's dreams to life. And though, as creators, we were born to bring our dreams into form, it's easy to default towards societal models of achievement that emphasize effort, manipulation, and force. As I've walked my own path of awakening, I've had many moments when I've naively attempted to force a goal or desire. But thankfully, I now have a much more mature understanding of how manifestation works.

We talked before about inner purpose and outer purpose. Your inner purpose is to align with who you truly are and to live an adventurous and wondrous life filled with expansion and joy. Your outer purpose is to live from that place of alignment as you express all dimensions of who you are by freely sharing your gifts, radiance, beauty, and magnificent "beingness" with the world. As you align with the True You, you are able to tune to the voice of your soul, which clearly knows your mission and purpose. And as you tune, your dreams and goals will begin to emanate from this pure place. They are no longer sourced from insecurities, lack and fear, or a desire to please others. They are soul-sourced and born from within.

Bearing this in mind, we can extrapolate a few things. First, our souls are aligned with the Mind of God. We are extensions of the Universe, all flowing from a single source of consciousness. As such, anything birthed from a pure place of alignment is essentially emanating from the Mind of God or Source itself, as it chooses to express itself through us. In this regard, God doesn't need any help birthing the dreams that were placed in us to begin with. All that's needed is for us to not get in our own way. Our only job is to align with who we are and to follow the moment-by-moment guidance that we receive as we journey on our way. So, to bring our dreams to life, we don't need to chase them down and wrestle them into reality. We can hold them with an effortless knowing that a partnership with the Universe renders them already done.

This is in line with how I've come to understand prayer. Before, my prayers were misguided and needy. There was a beseeching and pleading as I would petition God to give me what I thought that I needed or wanted. Now I understand that the purpose of prayer is not to move or change the Mind of God, which is already perfect in its knowing, but rather to attune ourselves to that which has already been established for our good. So, whether the desire is a dream house that would delight me or a financial goal, by the time it lands in my mind and heart, I can receive it as a reality that I only need to attune to and allow, with ease and grace. All the while trusting that it will be delivered in the perfect time and in the perfect way.

Our society leans heavily towards an unbalanced masculine energy, which is characterized by action, conquest, dominance, and control. As such, we are encouraged to doggedly pursue our goals and "make" things happen. Our language even celebrates this determined machismo, using words and phrases like "killed it," "slayed," and "dominated" to describe another's success. But this preponderance towards forced action runs counter to the makings of the Universe, which flows in rhythmic, balanced, and effortless ways.

When we walk the path of awakening, we don't have to rely on our own might. We can leverage the power of the Universe, which knows our dreams and the best way to bring them to pass. Furthermore, it knows the countless ways that our desires can unfold. When we cling and grab and force and pull, we only get in our way and slow our flow. Aligned action, which presents as inspired ideas that come from a place of alignment, is always encouraged, but aligned action feels different than forced action. Forced action zaps our strength and eventually leads to burn-out, exhaustion, and oftentimes, frustration. By contrast, aligned action is regenerative, life-giving, easy, and sustainable.

Over the last few years, I have been ever so mindful of these differences as I unpack and play with my own dreams. Even as I write, in this very moment, I'm witnessing a dream unfold with the physical space that I'm in. One of the things I've wanted for some time was a space in our home to call my own, but no matter what plan I pursued, I just couldn't seem to figure it out. I would go back and forth with my husband petitioning for certain configurations, but it would always feel like I was forcing a solution. One clear sign to me, when my husband is involved, is whether there is a spirit of harmony between us. Again, if it feels like force, then I know that it's me trying to make something happen. So, in this case, recognizing that I had to push way too much, I pulled back. Hands off... which signals, "Universe, I'm turning this over to you."

Recently, a series of events unfolded over a few months that landed me in the perfect room in the house that is now being converted into my office/she space. And it started with my husband taking the lead to make it happen. First, one space opened. Then, this person shifted, and another space opened. Long story short, the largest upstairs bedroom is being renovated as my she-cave. And every detail has felt effortless, intentional, and blessed. My sister-in-law, who's design and imaging company is called "Joy Echo," is designing and styling my space. And she has blown me away with her ability to detail touches that make my heart sing. Both the process and space have truly been infused with joy. And my brother, who's a contractor, is lovingly executing on the vision that she's created. Easy, grace-filled, and wonderful.

I've also had similar experiences with other dreams, including things like travel and special events or experiences. If the desire felt like it was coming from a pure place, I would move myself out of the way and say, "Okay, Universe, if this is meant to be, make it so." My job then, was to follow the energy and guidance and to "allow" the details to unfold versus forcing them. Oftentimes, this would include not knowing when and how resources would come together and just surrendering and trusting the process. And I can tell you that whenever I've insisted on *only* following paths that carried a spirit of ease, the Universe has delivered.

Spiritual Goal Setting

"A good traveler has no fixed plans and is not intent on arriving."
– Lao Tzu

E ase, flow, allowance, grace. If this is the path and the Universe already knows our desires, should we even be concerned with setting goals? Should we just float through life? And how do we learn to follow the guidance laid out for us as we journey towards our dreams? We've established that our purpose is to live a life of expansion and joy, allowing the divine to express itself through us. In many ways, it's as if we raised our hands to volunteer for a delicious expedition headed to earth. If you think of the traveler who sets out on an excursion, maybe even as a vacation, they may set goals for different sites that they want to see, restaurants they'd like to experience, people they'd like to see, etc. However, if they hold too tightly to those plans, their vacation will likely end in frustration. For we know that even the best plans sometimes run into roadblocks. For example, you arrive at the restaurant you'd been dying to experience only to find that they are closed on Sundays.

Or perhaps, you miss the ferry that was to take you to the fabulous excursion you'd planned for the afternoon. Life happens. But if you travel while holding your plans loosely, you will likely not only get to check off a number of the items on your planned itinerary, but you will probably have some delicious, unexpected adventures as well. Plus, as good travel does, you will likely return home having grown a bit on the inside from discovering things about the world out there and the world inside yourself.

This life adventure is no different than that. Our goals simply give us a reason to be out in the world, finding our way towards remembering who we are. As we rendezvous with one another, we discover truths about ourselves and others that lead to our continued unfolding. Everything is about our spiritual expansion. Every encounter. Every experience. So, take from wisdom delivered to me by the international teacher and minister Reverend Deborah L. Johnson, "Set the goal, but just for the purpose of getting you in action." And, as you move forward, remember these core essentials, (1) detach from the need for a specific outcome, (2) focus on the joy of the journey and all that you are becoming because of it, (3) release the need to know how things will unfold, and (4) trust that the Universe is aware of your dreams and knows how best to deliver.

Accepting Where You Are

Another fundamental element involved with learning to flow with life is the art of accepting where you are. This is one of the foundational components of manifestation. Our desires must be steadied by a contentment with what is, even and especially when where we are is uncomfortable.

In 2016, right after the presidential election in the U.S., I had the great fortune of participating in a ten-day silent meditation retreat. The country had erupted as everyone grappled with the election results, and I had never been more ready to invite silence. During the retreat, we would begin each day at 4:30 a.m. in meditation, and we would meditate for approximately ten hours per day, breaking only for meals and a brief period in the afternoon for chores. This was a combination of group meditations in the meditation hall and private meditation in our rooms.

The style of meditation that we learned is called "vipassana," which is believed to be the form of meditation taught by the Buddha. With attention on the breath, practitioners sit upright in posture and focus on consciously scanning their bodies from head to toe, learning to feel the sensations that arise without judgment or reaction. The meditation hall was often chilly at times, and given that this was mid-December, we were provided with blankets and cushions to sit comfortably on the floor. But comfort, for me, was a bit elusive. At the time, I had to be mindful of my back to avoid pain, my allergies were flared, making it difficult to breathe through my nose (a fundamental component of this style of meditation), and I was in the thick of raging hot flashes. I remember being so uncomfortable that I went to the meditation teachers to discuss my various issues, and they kindly encouraged me to buck up and allow the process to unfold. They believed in my capacity to do what needed to be done.

On day five of the retreat, we shifted to a new phase called "Adhitthana," which translates as "sittings of strong determination." Prior to that point, as we sat, we were able to shift and reposition ourselves on the floor as necessary, which helped considerably. Sometimes, a slight shift might relieve a pain in my back. Or if a hot flash came while I was layered under multiple blankets, I could ease them off and continue meditating. However, Adhitthana required more. At this point, we were asked to be completely still as we meditated, not shifting in any way during the 45-minute group sittings. Strong determination. At first, I literally thought I would die. The request not to respond to an itch here or a sensation there was one thing, but asking me to sit and not move while enduring significant pain and discomfort was another. But I did it. I practiced and practiced, and I did it. By breathing and placing my full attention on repeatedly moving my awareness from my head to my toes and back again, I learned how to sit peacefully through the discomfort, acknowledging it but not needing to react to it.

The lessons from my experience with the retreat were broad and profound, but the most life-changing element was certainly my learning to embrace the sweet state of equanimity. Equanimity is a state of psychological composure and stability that is undisturbed by external stimuli. It's the ability to remain balanced and composed, even in stressful situations. In other words, it's learning to be okay with what is and doing so with dignity and grace.

During the retreat, there was a young lady who was a returning, practiced student who struck me in a profound way. I noticed in group meditations that she always sat so peacefully and gracefully, seeming never to be moved by anything that was happening in her and around her. After the retreat ended, I had an opportunity to engage with her, and I commented on how impressive she was. I had assumed that, given how still, grounded and composed she was, she must not have had any physical pain to contend with. However, in our conversation, she revealed that she actually carried unbelievable pain in a few areas of her body when she sat. Nevertheless, by practicing vipassana meditation, she had learned to sit peacefully and endure.

Lesson learned. We all have pain, whether physical, mental, or emotional. And we will always land in places where we experience varying degrees of discomfort. However, as we practice the art of acceptance and embrace the precepts of equanimity, we can learn to be grounded, still, and okay. And as we do, we are able to move out of the Universe's way so it can do its great work in us, through us, and for us.

The Essentials
of Wayfinding

"Would you tell me, please, which way I ought to go from here?"
"That depends a good deal on where you want to get to."
"I don't much care where –"
"Then it doesn't matter which way you go."
– LEWIS CARROLL, ALICE IN WONDERLAND

Filmmaker and anthropologist Elizabeth Lindsey is the first female and first Polynesian to serve as a fellow with the National Geographic Society. Her work takes her to remote parts of the world as she studies indigenous wayfinders to both understand and preserve their knowledge. Wayfinding relates to ways that people orient themselves to find their way from place to place. And we know, based on the work of researchers like Lindsey, that for centuries, ancient mariners from various cultures throughout the world were able to sail thousands of miles across the ocean without maps and instruments. These masterful navigators took their cues from nature itself by noting things like the rising and setting of the sun, the color of the clouds, the flight patterns of birds, or the patterns of movement in the ocean. They also cultivated their own inner stillness, which strengthened their ability to attune with nature. Many of their ways were passed down, and Lindsey travels to sit with wise elders who stand as keepers of this great knowledge. In an interview that I listened to with Lindsey, she talked about how the wayfinders explained that when they are sailing to an island, what they are doing is harnessing their internal power in such a way that they are actually calling the island to themselves. By learning to listen to nature around them and within, they would receive guidance on which path to take.

As I've navigated my life on what I consider to be a conscious, spiritual path, I have tapped into the services of many to help me find my way. i.e., coaches, ministers, astrologers, intuitives, and healers of many different types. But I am clear that if there's no one and nothing around me, I want to ensure that I have the means and capacity to find my own way. Therefore, I intentionally cultivate my own wayfinding abilities. And I do believe that this is how it's intended to be. Ultimately, we do not want to be dependent on anything outside of ourselves as we make our way on our respective journeys. Indeed, the ultimate goal is to learn to attune to our own inner guidance and take our cues from the Universe. And just as it is with the wise wayfinders, as we cultivate our inner power by using stillness, quietude, visioning, and other tools, we begin to call our goals and desires, or our "islands," to ourselves. Clarity comes, and the way is made clear, for when we're in alignment, our ability to perceive is enhanced. Furthermore, we can navigate life without pushing and depleting our life force. Moving from grit to grace.

Just now, I wanted to revisit the interview that I'd heard with Elizabeth Lindley, which I hadn't listened to in a very long time, maybe a couple of years. I pulled it up and realized that it was an hour and forty-one minutes. Not wanting to listen to the whole interview for the short segment that I wanted to hear, I decided to try my hand at finding it by jumping around. As I moved my hand to the player, I silently prayed, "Please help me find the right part." And on the first attempt, I landed on the exact segment. I called this little island to myself. No pushing. No force. Just the fruits of flow and sweet grace.

Following the Signs

So, as wayfinders, how do we know the signs? What do they look like? You'll know them when you attune to them, and they are always everywhere. Our challenge is never that there is a lack of signs along our path. Our challenge is that the lack of stillness within us often renders them invisible. A mind that's consumed with the past or the future cannot detect the gifts that are being offered in the present. As you awaken and align, you will start to notice the smallest of ways that the Universe is speaking to you. And this will become your evidence of how loved, adored, and worthy you truly are.

You're watching the TV, and the answer to something you've been struggling with pours out of an actor's mouth. You open a book, and your eyes land on a passage that offers the exact revelation you needed. You're driving down the street, and the license plate on the car in front of you has the perfect message. You turn your radio on, and the lyrics of a song illuminate your mind. You're standing in line at the grocery store, and the person in front of you turns out to have the perfect resource for a problem you'd been trying to resolve. This is how the Universe speaks, and this barely scratches the surface. I am always amazed by the deliciousness of the signs and the ways that they make their way into my awareness. And because what we focus on expands, the more we pay attention to them, the more we are flooded with these types of experiences.

One of my favorites happened last year. I dialogue with my soul all the time, and though I know it might sound nuts, sometimes, I even sing songs to myself. A few months back, I heard the Jackson Five's "I Wanna Be Where You Are," and I found the lyrics so precious that I began signing it to my soul. The tune is a love song and the core message for the object of Jackson's attention is, "wherever you are, that's where I'm trying to be too."

My goal was to send the message that the only place I wanted to be was at home inside of myself, guided by the truest and highest version of me.

Well, one morning, I was humming the tune in my head, totally feeling powerful and aligned, and I believe that I had a fleeting thought... not even fully formed... that went out as an invitation for my soul to speak back to me. When I got in the car, headed to work, I turned on Pandora radio, not a playlist, and the first song that played was Jackson Five's "I'll be There." I received this as my soul's reassurance that as I committed to being wherever it was, it would indeed "be there," waiting for me with open arms. It felt like the sweetest and most love-filled hug from the divine.

Another example. Recently, I was torn with whether I wanted to invest in adding a new tool to my coaching arsenal. It was not a significant investment or anything, but I just didn't know if it was right for me. Among other considerations, I've been mindful to watch for the sometimes-never-ending cycle of feeling like there's one more thing that we need in order to serve in the highest way. So, I was sitting with the decision before moving forward. And on this day, I decided that I was ready to finalize my decision either way. I sat on the couch and pulled out some books, including a notebook that I've been keeping with copious notes related to my work. As I was settling in, I said a simple prayer and asked to be clearly shown what to do. I let it go, moving on with my day, picked up my work notebook, and the very first words that I saw at the top of the page where I landed was a note I'd written, who knows how long ago, that said, "The True You stands on its own." That was my answer. I immediately felt it in my bones. This tool was not for me.

As you awaken and align, synchronicities and wonders will abound. Modern mystic Andrew Harvey says, "The more you wake up, the more you realize everything that's happening is a sign. Books open at the right place when you're beginning to become awake. You can be saved by messages you read in the sign on the road. You can be illuminated by somebody sitting next to you in a bus and humming a folk song that goes straight to the core of the problem..." Indeed, the signs are everywhere. And for those times when you feel confused and lost, just trust the process and lean on these words offered by my dear friend, Erika Harris, who says, "It is good to feel lost... because it proves you have a navigational sense of where Home is. You know that a place that feels like being found exists. And maybe your current location isn't that place but, Hallelujah, that unsettled, uneasy feeling of lost-ness just brought you closer to it."

Flow Power Tools

"To offer no resistance to life is to be in a state of grace, ease, and lightness. This state is then no longer dependent upon things being in a certain way, good or bad. It seems almost paradoxical, yet when your inner dependency on form is gone, the general conditions of your life, the outer forms, tend to improve greatly... Life flows with ease."
– Eckhart Tolle

Flow is about developing your capacity to move forward with ease and grace as you journey on your path. Whereas the power tools for Awaken and Align are aimed at bringing you into alignment with your True Self, Flow is about learning to leverage the power that comes from alignment. With it, the themes of allowing and letting go are paramount, as well as the admonition to be gentle with yourself and others along the way.

Power of Rituals

Having daily rituals that ground you is an essential part of achieving and maintaining a sense of flow. I recommend utilizing them in the morning and at night. In the morning, you can start with something as simple as stating an intention. This will set the tone for your day and create a powerful container for you to step into. I will always start my day with a prayer and intention. For more than a year now, the one that I use the most is this, *"Thank you for this day. Bless and guide me in it. Use me to serve your people. And with every interaction, let there be love."* It shapes my day, reminds me to dwell in my purpose, and helps me to remember the point of it all... love.

Other ideas for rituals include spiritual baths, using tools such as crystals and essential oils, meditation, journaling, and visualization, all of which can be done any time of day. What I call "bath therapy" is a daily practice for me. I indulge in luxurious bath products (truly nurturing my mind, body, and spirit) and utilize a variety of practices, from chanting with mala beads to visualizations and meditations while in the tub. Water is extremely healing and nurturing and is thought to connect us with the spiritual realm.

Power of Visualization

For years, psychologists have recommended visualization to support people with enhancing their skills, improving their emotional states, and realizing their goals. Visualization works in many ways, but primarily, it tells the brain which direction to move in by giving it clear imagery. When done effectively, it signals the subconscious mind and puts it to work towards the intended goal. Metaphysically, visualization raises your vibration, gets you out of your own way, and allows the Universe to do its work. You can use guided imagery or ramp up your own imagination. The goal is to engage all your senses as much as possible as you imagine the desired outcome of a situation. You can also simply visualize peace, health, and happiness coming to you, those you love, and the entire world.

Power of Release

In order to flow, it's necessary to remain buoyant, and to be buoyant, you must release the weights. Whatever the challenge, offer it to the divine as often as necessary. Release judgment, anger, resentment, or anything that lowers your vibration and keeps you out of alignment. Let it go. Also, release your attachment to when and how you believe your dreams and goals should manifest. You can use visualization to help you release whatever needs to be released. Imagine it in your mind's eye and see yourself offering it to God or letting it go in some other way. Send it down the stream. See it vanish inside a ball of light. Watch it float away into the heavens. Oftentimes, during moments that call for surrender, I will start humming the title words of an old gospel song called, "I Surrender All." It's a simple little, precious tune, and it works wonders.

I also routinely enjoy the traditional Chinese medicine of acupuncture and cupping, and I often use the treatments as a time of energetic release.

Flow Reflective Questions

"Live one day at a time. Keep your attention in the present time. Have no expectations. Make no judgements. And give up the need to know why things happen."
– CAROLYN MYSS

1. *In your life, what evidence is there that you may be holding on to resentment and animosity?*

2. *How has holding on to losses and regrets affected your life?*

3. *Do you carry any stories of personal suffering and injustice that have been difficult for you to let go? How do these stories shape your identity? Who would you be without them?*

4. *Are you clinging too tightly to a goal or dream? What would it feel like to let it go and put it in the hands of the Universe?*

5. *Is there something in your life for which you carry shame? What would it take for you to forgive yourself?*

6. *Do you know the voice of your soul? How does it speak to you?*

7. *What types of synchronicities have you noticed in your life? Are you ready to invite more?*

Flow Soul Qualities

Resilience

"I can be changed by what happens to me.
But I refuse to be reduced by it."
– MAYA ANGELOU

When we first moved into our current home, we had ten red oak trees planted in our back yard. Once seedlings, they now all stand about 25 feet tall, some thin and wispy, some thick and majestic. When it storms, I sometimes enjoy watching them, noticing how they bear the harsh winds and rains... trunks bending, leaves violently twirling, but always springing back with grace and beauty, even if they've lost a limb or two. We see this quality of resilience in animals as well and even babies and small children. Once, our friends' son took a tumble down our stairs when he was about three years old, and we were amazed by how quickly he bounced back up and kept moving, unphased by his significant stumble. It's as if those creatures and beings that know nothing beyond living in the now, are indeed the most resilient. They lack the capacity to lament their misfortunes. They just bounce back, keep moving, and keep right on shining.

Resilience is one of my favorite soul qualities. It's intertwined with the belief that not only do we have the capacity to survive challenging situations, but we also grow from them, somehow landing better than we were before. Resilience is learning to master that natural sense of buoyancy that we spoke about under the "Power of Release." Those who are resilient can bounce back from trials and tribulations because they maintain a fierce focus on the now, not holding on to regrets and disappointments about the past and not holding on to judgments about themselves, life, and others. They are flexible, optimistic, and lighthearted, not taking themselves or life too seriously.

Humility

"I believe that the first test of a great man is his humility. I don't mean by humility, doubt of his power. But really great men have a curious feeling that the greatness is not of them, but through them. And they see something divine in every other man and are endlessly, foolishly, incredibly merciful."
– JOHN RUSKIN

Humility is being grounded equally in your humanity and divinity. It's having an accurate view of who you are, both in terms of understanding your human frailties as well as your eternal connection to the powerful reserves of the Universe. Unfortunately, humility is sometimes misunderstood and perceived as a weakness. However, true humility is one of the most powerful dimensions of the True You. Humility is having a quiet confidence and strength. It's being teachable and moldable and stands as the opposite of bravado and force, deriving its power, instead, from its rootedness in stillness and truth. It is a quality that resonates with others because it carries with it a spirit of deference. You know your power, but you also know that it originates beyond you.

When you are in flow, living as the True You, you know that you are tapped into a greater source. Nothing feels more wonderful and exhilarating than being immersed in a task or activity and sensing that something greater is sourcing through you and doing the work. Having had this experience, only the arrogant or ignorant would stand with a false pride and ownership of what was birthed. Humility is the wise part within us that, upon creating or witnessing beauty, points to God. I love music, and I remember, at one point, being so moved by "The Prayer" (performed by Celine Dion and Andrea Bocelli) that I did a quick search to see if I could find out more about how it came to be. Sure enough, I came across a passage where David Foster, the composer, described it as, "... a song that I just never get tired of playing, I never get tired of hearing it, and I never get tired of people telling me that they enjoy it... I think it came through me... it's very meaningful to me that when all is said and done, there is a piece of music like that, that will undoubtedly outlive me. It was a moment—that song was a moment for sure." "It came through me" ... these are words that point to that something greater.

So, when we read Matthew 5:5, "Blessed are the meek, for they will inherit the earth," we understand why. The meek (or humble) are those who walk lightly upon the earth, beautifying it by tapping into a power that lights the world, but never claiming it as their own.

PART IV:
LOVE

Our Now Moment, Choosing Love

"Love is the essence of All That Is, no matter what we do here, we are met with love. We also feel how our choices were in alignment or out of alignment with that love."
– SUZANNE GIESEMANN

At the writing of this book, we are nearing the final quarter of 2020, a year that has been like no other. The entire world was forced to pause in unprecedented ways as a pandemic landed at our door. And from there, our losses seemed to multiply. In addition to losing more than one million people to the virus worldwide, it has disrupted the global economy and met with other challenges, in what, at times, has felt like the "perfect storm." In the U.S., the pandemic seemed to elucidate our systemic frailties, exposing a feeble healthcare system, inequities in our education system, as well as deep-rooted racial and economic disparities. Add to this civil unrest, fueled by racial injustice, and a political climate that has left the nation standing at dangerous levels of polarization, and we are forced to conclude that something quite mysterious is brewing.

Anyone observing all of this at ground zero, the level of the virtual explosion, is probably so mired in the details that they are likely feeling overrun with grief and despair. After all, it feels like the world is "going to hell in a handbasket," as the old folks used to say. And we haven't even touched on concerns regarding the viability of the earth itself.

As I've watched things unfold from where I stand, I've wanted to gather up as many people as I can, lather them in love, and reassure them, while hugging them fiercely, that, "It's all okay." You see, if 2020 had landed ten or fifteen years ago... or maybe even a year or two ago, I may have been amongst those stuck in the depths of despair. If concerns about my family's capacity to stay healthy amid the pandemic didn't take me out, then surely the pain from racial injustice and the ugliness of our political landscape would. Yep, the veiled Monica Moody would probably have been at the edge of frenzy.

But thankfully, I am blessed to have stepped onto a path of awakening that, in perfect timing, led me to a place where I have gained enough elevation to view the current scene from a much higher perspective. Lifted by grace, the True Me is wise enough to know that what's unfolding must be viewed with the god glasses on.

In his book "A New Earth," Eckhart Tolle explains that we are at the point in the evolution of consciousness where, if we want to enjoy the continuity of humanity, our awakening is no longer an option. The effects of our collective choices, under the guidance of the dysfunctional ego, are essentially catching up with us and leading to our potential destruction. As such, we find ourselves at a crossroad moment where we must make a definitive choice about who and what we want to be. Tolle explains, "When faced with a radical crisis, when the old way of being in the world, of interacting with each other and with the realm of nature doesn't work anymore, when survival is threatened by seemingly insurmountable problems, an individual life-form – or a species – will either die or become extinct or rise above the limitations of its condition through an evolutionary leap."

Everything about where we are right now reeks of "radical crisis," and as Tolle explains, the old ways of being simply do not work anymore. Furthermore, if I was a betting woman, I would suppose that the bottom, in this unfolding saga, is just starting to fall out. But this is where the god glasses come in handy. We started this written journey together with me explaining how the awakening process is often precipitated by pain. The Universe whispers, then it incrementally ups the volume on its voice, moving towards the blazoned shout if necessary, to gain our attention. And if that doesn't work, the next step is what feels like a violent and disruptive shaking. We are in the midst of that shaking, and it's time for us to awaken to the truth of who we are. And as we awaken at the level of the individual, our awakened consciousness will then be reflected in our collective experience. We are in the middle of our own shared moment of grace, and what we do with it is completely up to us. If we want to make the leap and birth a more beautiful world, then we must each do our part as midwives of our collective future.

If you've made it to this point in the book, then you are most assuredly on a conscious path of awakening, for your arrival to this juncture is an indication that you have found resonance with at least some parts of what I've shared. In this sense, our remaining conversation is not so much about finding the light as much as it is about amplifying it. The True You is on the scene, and though you have clearly unleashed it, it is now beckoning you to take an even greater leap towards love. How do I know this? Because it's what the Universe is asking of all of us. As we move through Awaken, Align, and Flow, the next phase of the model, on the road to transformation, is Love.

This is a profound moment of spiritual transformation on the planet. The time for the evolutionary leap that Tolle spoke of is now.

And the only way to call forth the world that we desire in our hearts is to be it. Just like the indigenous wayfinders, we must attune to our inner power and hold the vision of it so strongly that we call it to ourselves. We must return to our true nature and *be* whatever we feel is missing from this world and call it forth. This is the way of the masters, like Buddha and Jesus. Jesus believed in the well-being of others so profoundly that he called it forth. We too have this capacity, but to access it, we must engage in the practice of love. We use our spiritual tools to open our hearts and heal our minds, and then, we live love.

This is so profoundly important that I have chosen to dedicate Part IV to detailing what it looks like to live as the True You in key areas of your life. That is, what it looks like to lean towards love, embodying it as a transformative state of being. It is important that we understand what the conscious spiritual path looks like in plain clothes. But before we move to this part of the discussion, it's necessary to explore a foundational component of love.

May Grace Be
My First Response

"Grace is that ability; to face adversity and be at ease, to enter into the suffering world and help others without losing yourself in the process. It is to be true to your most essential nature, and produce something good from that. To have grace is as close as we may come to perfection."
– Christopher Daniel Mechling

A few months ago, due to a story that was cycling on social media, I found myself having to console one of my daughters as she tried not to completely succumb to fear behind things that were brewing in the world. I spent about half an hour speaking life into her mind and heart and reminding her of her power.

Ironically, a few minutes before that, I'd taken a conscious moment to tune in to what was happening in the U.S. with so many burdened by current events. And my heart was already leaning towards wanting to support those who were reeling from pain. With so much happening right now, if we don't get clear on how we can respond in a way that simultaneously meets our needs and the needs of the world, then we will all be overrun by grief and fear. Because regardless of what anyone says, we cannot be of service and we cannot live the lives we were intended to live if we feel broken, worn, and afraid.

So, how do we move through all of this? What do we do with everything that's brewing right now? What do we do when a dozen things equally feel like the greatest challenge of our lives? I'd first like to submit that our greatest challenge does not fall on the list of those things that are seemingly obvious. Our greatest challenge is much more subtle and easier to miss.

We think that our greatest challenge is surviving this pandemic and figuring out a way to work, create, and live in the face of it. We think that our greatest challenge is righting systems and structures that have fallen out of balance and failed us in countless ways. We think that our greatest challenge is figuring out a way to live on this beautiful earth without depleting and destroying it. We think that our greatest challenge is finding strong, conscious leaders we can trust to operate in the best interests of those they serve. We think that our greatest challenge is creating a world that is just and fair for brown and black people, a world where we can exist with the same rights, freedoms, and sense of safety and well-being that whites enjoy. But our greatest challenge is none of these things.

Our greatest challenge is learning to hold space for all the things that we care about in a way that does not demand that we surrender our peace and power. Our greatest challenge is learning how to stand for a cause without having to live in a constant state of anger, grief, and disbelief. It's possible to be moved but not mangled. Stirred but not shaken. Aware but not afraid. Whether it's fear of a pandemic or fear for the lives of black and brown people, fear is fear, and it robs the soul of who you are. Further, it prevents you from seeing possibilities that are available to you and renders you powerless to effect change.

This is a mountaintop moment. If you stay in the valley of fear, you will collapse from the weight of it all. But if you journey towards higher ground, you will be able to see things with greater clarity.

> *"For God hath not given us the spirit of fear; but of power,*
> *and of love, and of a sound mind."*
> – 2 TIMOTHY 1:7

We don't have to walk through this world cowering and afraid. I will not spend my days worrying about racial injustice and the safety of my black girls and my black nieces and nephews. I will bless them and put their hands in the hand of the Creator and know that they will not have an encounter or experience that is not a part of their divine path. And at night, I will rest knowing that I serve them best when I hold them in the light of love, not in the shadows of fear.

I invite you to do the same thing. Sit with God for a while and ask, "In this moment, what is required of me? How can I serve without losing myself, my peace, my joy?" Sit it down. Release the weightiness of every situation and thought that binds your mind and your heart and breathe. Breathe deeply and then breathe some more. And as you breathe, allow your mind to settle down and regain its balance so your heart can then hear the guidance of your soul.

But don't be surprised if your soul directs you to just be. Being an energetic mountain of peace is just as powerful as leading a revolution. They both have a place in what's unfolding.

Even if I don't openly join public discourse about the latest situation or event, you best believe that I am spiritually attuned to what is happening and doing my part to ensure that the world doesn't completely tip over into fear. I am doing the quiet work that I have been called to do.

I've learned that I don't have to assume the weight of this world to show my solidarity, support, and love. I don't have to walk with worry as my partner to demonstrate that I care. Even when my girls are hurt and suffering, I will not join them in their pain. Two hurting souls who feel hopeless will not move anything, let alone mountains. So, when they are feeling weary and worn, I compassionately hold space for them to remember who they are and find their way back to their place of power. I did it that night as my daughter's tears soaked my pajamas. I called on the forces of grace to hold both me and her.

If you haven't detected it by now, "grace" is one of my favorite words. I just did a check as I write, and I've used it a total of 53 times. Though not intentional, it is just a core word in a new language for the new world we have been asked to birth. Grace is so many things, but for this part of our conversation, let's spotlight it as the ability to be at ease with the situations that unfold in our lives and in the world. As Christopher Daniel Mechling noted in the quote above, it's being true to your most essential nature and producing good from that. The path of awakening has revealed that all things are working together for our good, even when we don't see how. As such, our task is to trust the process and focus, at all times, on simply being who we have been called to be.

We have been conditioned to think that the way to create change in our lives and in the world is by taking massive action. But I submit that the most powerful way to create change is to *be*. We live in a vibrational Universe. Everything is energy. When you are being the True You, you are radiating a vibration of peace, freedom, joy, and love. And because the Universe must reflect what you are being, this returns as good in your life and reverberates into the world. This is how we create the new Earth.

With your god glasses on, you can maintain an awareness that things are unfolding as a part of a divine plan and rest easy, without losing yourself in the details of what's happening, whether it be in your own private life or on the world stage. Let grace be your first response. You don't have to push against anything. You don't have to bear undue burdens. Surrender. Be love. And follow the guidance of your soul... on all matters. Nothing is excluded from the grace that we learn to offer the world through our own alignment. And through this, we begin to bear witness to the power and influence that we have in our efforts when they are channeled from a place of love.

Self-Love

"She practiced self Love until her self became Love.
At last, she was free."
– JAIYA JOHN

I am a black woman who was raised in a conservative Christian household in America. Before I could even gain my footing in the world, I was taught that sacrificing myself was a requirement to get ahead. Work hard. Be strong. Deny yourself. Submit to your husband. Squelch those sinful desires. Put your kids first. Don't make black folks look bad. Give to your community. Don't be too emotional. Don't let them see you sweat. And with whatever's left... change the world. Never was it a conversation about honoring my truths, taking care of myself, and loving all parts of me.

We live in a culture that celebrates self-sacrifice as a virtue, and this has caused many to adopt a mindset and lifestyle that leaves them depleted and unfulfilled. As I have awakened to the truth of who I am, I've had to unlearn many ways of being and replace them with a holistic framework that confidently places me at the center of my own world. I suspect that this statement may make you cringe a little because it's so foreign to what we've been told about how to hold ourselves. You may be thinking, "How selfish! How egotistical!" But the world was made for me, just as it was made for all of us. "A Course in Miracles" says, "All of the children of God are special, and none of the children of God are special." We are all equal. We are all special. And none of us is more or less deserving than another. That includes me. And that includes you.

You are here to experience a life of joy. That joy is derived from expressing your true nature and being the True You. It's derived from prioritizing your needs and doing things that enliven your soul. It's derived from caring for yourself physically, mentally, emotionally, and spiritually. It's derived from practicing forgiveness and compassion towards yourself. It's derived from accepting your flaws and embracing your tender places. When you open to the truth of who you are, what you'll find standing there in the middle of your own heart is you. You are love. And before you can genuinely give it to another, you must first authentically and powerfully own it for yourself.

The beauty that comes from loving you first is you then position yourself to radiate that love more powerfully into the world. When you tend to your own needs first, you are able to maintain higher levels of vibration by staying in alignment with the True You. Think about it. It's hard to be clear-minded when you are physically exhausted. It's in the stillness of a replenished and restful place that our perceptions are clear. And when our perceptions are clear, we see things through the eyes of our souls.

So, honor yourself and lavish yourself with love. If you're tired, rest. If you want space, be alone. If your body needs attention, nurture it. Learning to listen to the guidance of your soul is the first part. Heeding that guidance is the next. Learn to trust your own intuitive knowing about what you need to fully care for you.

One of my favorite platforms on social media is the Nap Ministry, an interactive, social resistance project headed by performance artist and poet Tricia Hersey. Hersey declares herself as the Bishop of this ministry aimed at bringing awareness to the dangers of grind culture by "spreading the gospel of rest." Though my views differ from some of the tenets espoused by the platform, I do hold a fundamental agreement about the power and sanctity of rest. These are a few of my favorite quotes from Hersey's ministry:

> *"Your obsession with productivity as a function of your worth*
> *is preventing you from tending to your soul. Naps are soul care."*

> *"Modern society tells us that we don't have enough.*
> *We aren't doing enough. All lies.*
> *We have enough of everything, including time.*
> *Grind culture has created a pace that*
> *has taken away our DREAMSPACE.*
> *We can restore it. We will rest."*

What I love most about Hersey's work is that it stands as evidence of a shifting narrative that illuminates shared, false beliefs about how we must navigate this world and it gives us permission to return to practices that honor the soul of who we are.

At this point in my life, I live by a simple rule as it relates to my own self-love and self-care, and that's this... If what's being asked of me does not serve me, then it's impossible for it to fully serve another. Because if I am diminished as I offer whatever it is, then it's not being delivered with love.

Love In Relationships

"Each person you meet is an aspect of yourself,
clamoring for love."
– ERIC MICHA'EL LEVENTHAL

The day I realized that I didn't have to wait for others to change to be happy is the day that I was born anew. When I think about all of the time that was lost, being mad at someone because of something they did or didn't do or being disappointed with someone because they didn't live up to my expectations, I am truly humbled. In my younger years, and even the not-too-distant past, I would wrestle with others, especially those I love the most, to try to get them to see things my way or shift from whatever behaviors I perceived to be causing me pain. Even now, I still must watch for this when it rears its head in sneaky and suspicious ways. The ego wants us to control things out there, which always includes others. The soul, by contrast, wants to master things from within.

Relationships, like everything else, reflect our inner world. So, anytime we are experiencing discomfort from a relationship, that pain is reflecting something about our own choices and beliefs. This is a good thing because it puts the ball in our court. Instead of giving away our power, we learn to release others from the bondage of needing to set us free. That's love.

A few years ago, while hosting my great big old tribe on the 4th of July, an unfortunate family incident erupted. Due to flared egos and a trail of misunderstandings, my clan experienced a terrible break. Right down the middle it seemed, yielding two distinct factions. I was devastated. Though I was not directly involved in the entanglement, I was terribly bereaved. And to my own amazement, I experienced the weightiness of grief. Because I felt that irreparable harm had been done, I had trouble releasing the situation and finding my way to the light. Furthermore, I realized that I had some strong beliefs about who needed to do what to make things right.

It took a couple of years, but we eventually made our way back, and for that, I am so, so grateful. But even more than that, I am grateful for the lessons learned. The first thing I learned was the incredible power of setting people free of my judgment and expectations. Next, I learned that we are all doing the best we know, based on our own level of consciousness. In other words, we are all just trying to find our way. And finally, I learned as philosopher Marcus Aurelius so beautifully stated in a quote that I previously shared, "If you are distressed by anything external, the pain is not due to the thing itself, but to your estimate of it; and this you have the power to revoke at any moment." I am so glad that this situation pushed me into grief because ultimately, I learned that it wasn't the situation that actually did the pushing; it was my "estimate of it." Personal power... restored.

Our relationships are often our greatest teachers. We bump into each other almost daily, not realizing that there's gold in each of those bumps. Over the years, I've learned a lesson or two about what love looks like in relationships, and I offer these insights to you:

You'll See What You're Looking For

We learned before that whatever we give our attention to expands in our awareness. This holds true in our relationships as well. My husband is an incredible person, and yet, there was a point in our relationship where I took his good qualities for granted and focused primarily on those things that I found problematic. I wasn't doing it consciously, but inevitably, I was always much more vocal about the things that he did "wrong." One day, he had just gotten home from work, and sure enough, I immediately brought something negative to his attention. I was the nagging wife without even trying. On this day, overwhelmed by my constant judgments, he said, "You know, everyone thinks I'm a pretty good person except for you." My God. In an instant, I was changed. I realized that I had made it a habit of spotlighting any perceived negative quality or attribute in him that I could find, which was the opposite of what I wanted to do. From that point on, I worked on myself. My goal was to search for and amplify the good in him. And our relationship has gotten better and better. Now, this is my own secret little weapon. I don't do this just for my husband; I do it for everyone.

When we look for the best parts in others, that's what we find. And because the Law of Attraction is at work on every single front, it amplifies what we are focusing on and brings more of that to us. This is how we call forth the brilliance in others. We spotlight it. And it grows. Simultaneously, this choice to seek and find the good in others must also return to us. As you try it on, you will start to notice that others tend to find and spotlight the good in you, for indeed, we reap what we sow.

Be What You Feel is Missing

"A Course in Miracles" says, "Only what you are not giving can be lacking in any situation." This is a mind-boggling somersault of truth. If peace is absent, it's because you are not bringing it. If patience is lacking, it's because you are not offering it. When we lead with this belief, it absolves others of the need to be what we desire to experience for ourselves. In essence, the quote is on par with the famous quote by Gandhi that we must be the change we wish to see in the world. Play with this concept in your relationships. Be whatever you feel someone is not extending to you, and you'll have it.

Love Allows

Love in relationships feels free. It's not clingy, controlling, or manipulative. It honors the humanity in others and allows them to tread their own paths without interference and demands from us. Acceptance, allowance, compassion... grace. These are the felt qualities of love in any relationship. If at any point you feel the need to force someone to do something or be something in one of your relationships, know that this is a sign that the ego is at the helm, not the True You.

Furthermore, once released from the resistance of your demands, oftentimes, others will have the space and freedom to rise to who they are being called to be. Force creates counterforce. So, attempts to force anything on another, even if it's just your point of view, will often backfire. If you need an example of this, turn your attention to the current landscape that is American politics.

Boundaries are Compatible with Love

When we're on the path of awakening, we sometimes have to distance ourselves from people who take us out of alignment until we can build our spiritual muscles to a place where we are not thrown off by their presence in our lives. Learning to protect ourselves and establish healthy boundaries is an act of love. Boundaries are also necessary when someone has done something to cause us harm. Even if we acknowledge their lack of consciousness in their decisions and choices, this does not mean that we must continue to be in a relationship with them. Sometimes people can be so unconscious that all we can do is bless them from afar. Love is not feeble and unwise. It's possible to hold a compassionate "boundaried" love with others as we allow them to find their way.

Love in Parenting

"There are two gifts we should give our children.
One is roots. The other is wings."
– UNKNOWN

If you asked me to point to the most profound expression of grace in my life, I would quickly pull out a picture of my girls. I have two daughters, Taylor, 25, and Sydni, 17. Also, last year, the Universe saw fit to send a beautiful bonus daughter our way, Whitney, who's 16. Our girls are the most magnificent displays of human beings that you can imagine. They are loving, compassionate, open-minded, creative, intelligent women who are grounded, intuitive, change-makers. Over the years, we have received a host of feedback from people from different vantage points, commending us for raising such brilliant beings, with some even asking for tips and guidance on how to replicate our perceived work. And with every conversation, I humbly point to my favorite force, "grace."

They've always excelled in school, with an incredible propensity to work independently, without a whole lot of interference from us.

And my eldest has even captured two Ivy League degrees, one from Barnard College at Columbia University and a second from Harvard University. She's now working as a dance teacher with the goal of using dance to heal the hearts and minds of black and brown children. And as for Sydni, in addition to thriving academically, she is also a gifted soccer player and artist with her eyes on Stanford or Cal Arts. She is a leader among her friends with the wisdom of a sage.

And then there's Whitney, the soft-spoken, gentle giant and cheerleader who hasn't even begun to glimpse the depths of her power. But I see it. She too does well academically, and she's starting to find her leadership legs. When she's freely being her true self, she has an infectious presence that's ladled with joy. Yep, another world changer on deck.

With all of our girls, we have simply allowed love to lead the way in how we parent them. We hold space for their brilliance until they can know it and find it themselves. We remind them of their inherent power, refusing to see them as victims of anything. We exercise a gentle corrective style of parenting instead of a tyrannical, oppressive one. We allow them to make mistakes without adding layers of judgment. We encourage them to be considerate and compassionate towards others. And finally, we support them in owning their frailties by openly confessing and owning our own. Again, all by grace. We have made plenty of poor decisions along the way and failed in innumerable ways. But the thing that has powerfully undergirded our approach is the recognition that they are souls on their own journeys. They do not belong to us.

Love allows. And this is most certainly applicable in parenting. Our children are not here to mimic our beliefs. They aren't here to live our dreams. And they certainly aren't here to meet our expectations. They are here to live out their own purpose and mission, and the best thing that we could ever do is give them the space to chart their own soul led paths.

Love at Work

*"Work is love made visible. And if you cannot work with
love but only with distaste, it is better that you should leave
your work and sit at the gate of the temple and take alms of
those who work with joy."*

– KAHLIL GIBRAN

When I shifted to coaching full time, back in 2011, I was madly passionate about championing love in the workplace. So much so that my platform was called "Love at Work" with an adorable matching logo to boot. I recognized that if any place sat ripe and ready for more love and transformation, it was the world of work. And so, I set out to do what I could to create change. Trying to gain a historical understanding of how the work environment became so universally devoid of humanity, I did my research. And I determined that one primary issue was outdated notions about professionalism, which caused people to leave their full selves at the door.

Professionalism is defined as "the skill, good judgment, and polite behavior that is expected from a person who is trained to do a job well." No problems there at all. But, in our workplaces, I'm afraid that we have allowed a whole lot more to slip in under the guise of professionalism. Somewhere along the way, we bought into the notion that to be professional, we had to hide our humanity and detach from who we really are. This means to hide your weaknesses, be emotion-free, show very little personality, and keep the real you at bay.

As a Career Coach and a Trainer, I've worked with countless people who own and honor the fact that there's the one version of who they are that shows up at work and another that shows up for everything else. And there's a price to be paid for this. There's research that shows that moving through the world like transformers and expending our life force to fit in is taking a toll on our very well-being. That alone should serve as enough inspiration to drop with the masks and allow one integrated you to show up everywhere, including work. But there's another reason why only allowing segmented parts of yourself at work just won't work.... The True You is not having it.

Being the True You is about aligning with your best self or soul self and allowing that version to take the lead in ALL areas of your life. And that includes work. Your soul signature, i.e., unique divine expression, is meant to be blasted everywhere. That means your quirks, your humor, your honesty, your playfulness, your humanity, your joy ... whatever those things are that make you YOU, are wanted. And remember, have no fear because your commitment to the awakened path means that you will be constantly aiming for the best version of you. Not the egoic you, but the "soul on deck" you. And that version of you is fully workplace friendly.

So what does love at work look like? It's simple. Dare to be seen. Lead with your enthusiasm. Don't water it down. Bring your fun, joyful, loving self to work every day. Sprinkle generous words of praise to those who are doing good work. Help someone who may be afraid to ask for help. Release poisonous grudges and resentments. Be present and engaged with the people you serve. Be compassionate, vulnerable, and forgiving without worrying about being labeled as weak. Be generous with your kindness. Be empathetic and understanding. And release yourself and others from antiquated notions of professionalism that have nothing to do with one's abilities. Love at work looks like trust, respect, openness, support, accountability, fairness, honesty, connection, acceptance, passion, humor, and play. Give these things to others wherever you find yourself planted, and you will positively change the face of work as we know it.

In 2011, I hosted a weeklong event called "The Awaken Your Soul at Work Tele-summit," where I interviewed many of the heroes and sheroes who had supported my own awakening. Among them was Reverend Deborah L. Johnson, who I previously mentioned. Her wisdom and presence are always so powerful that I often find myself bowled over by her words. My personal interview with her was no different. It was one of the most impactful experiences I've had, and since then, I've shared that interview with many clients and friends. Though I'm obviously unable to share that interview in its entirety within the confines of this space, I would like to share my favorite part of Reverend Deborah's words about "work."

We have set up this false dichotomy in our mind where there's our life and there's our job. And we're not integrated. There's a me that goes to work that's different than the me that's walking around in the world. And what I would encourage people to do is try to close that gap... Don't wait 'til you get someplace else to be fully you. If you're willing to be fully you wherever you are, then THAT work environment will get transformed.

And when you look at work as an arena... not just a task of activities and responsibilities... but a forum, a stage, a laboratory... for your own personal growth and development and the healing of the world and the planet, you will see that there are all kinds of opportunities that are with you, right there, to truly make a difference, if we SHIFT what we think of as work.

Love and Money

> *"Money is like a river. It flows where the conditions are conducive to its flow."*
> – JACINTA MPALYENKANA

"For to the one who has, more will be given, and he will have an abundance, but from the one who has not, even what he has will be taken away." Matthew 13:12; I remember when I first really and truly understood this passage. It felt like such a gift. I realized that it's all about what happens both in the mind and heart. When we focus on the good in our lives, it expands, and more goodness flows in. And when we focus on what we perceive as a lack, even that will be taken away. The Universe will always bring us more of whatever we believe.

At the level of love, on our way towards mastery, we recognize that provision in every form, including money, is a given. The Universe is infinitely abundant, and we can access that abundance at any time by simply tuning to it. If our state of consciousness is hovering in lack, then that will be our experience. Conversely, if we are tuned to the abundance of what we already have, then more of it will come our way.

As we noted on the topic of dreams and desires, they chose you. What you want wants to be born through you. As Rumi declared, "What you seek is seeking you." The same holds true with money. It seeks to be used by you. That you have the desire for it is the evidence that it's already available to you. It already belongs to you. The goal then is to relax and trust that it will manifest when and as it's needed. The hardest part is to shift from "believing" this to truly "knowing" it, which is what we achieve at the level of Love. There's a point where the universe has proven itself in such powerful ways, so many times, that you no longer have doubt. You believe in your worthiness, and you trust that your well-being is always assured.

In the fascinating little book, "Dollars Want Me," published in 1903, the author, Henry Harrison Brown, explains our power and authority over money beautifully.

In regard to money, regard it also as merely the power that keeps business going. Welcome its coming and rejoice in its going. It never does its work until, like water in the stream, it has passed under the wheel. YOU alone are the Power. Money only has delegated power. You direct its expression. Change your attitude toward money. It is not the 'almighty dollar'. Almighty Power uses the dollar. Say to the dollar, 'I do not need you. You need me. You are of no use until my brain and hand use you. You wish to be used. You come to me that you may be used. I do not need a dollar. Dollars need me.' Assume this mental attitude and see what change it makes for you. When you have changed your aura, dollars will be drawn and you need not think of their coming.

In my own life, I am just at the point of teetering on this as a sustained level of awareness. I'm shifting from treating money like the pot of water where you are constantly checking to see if it's boiling, which is evidence of doubt and a lack consciousness, to knowing that it's already done. Love, in all areas of our lives, feels easy, sure, and abundant, and we must learn to manage our relationship with money in this same lighthearted way.

Love in Social Justice & Activism

"Someday, after mastering the winds, the waves, the tides and gravity, we shall harness for God the energies of love, and then, for a second time in the history of the world, man will have discovered fire."
– PIERRE TEILHARD DE CHARDIN

So how do we change the world at the level of love? With all that I've shared at this point, the answer to this question should be obvious. We change the world by choosing to be what we wish to see. We change the world by visioning what we desire and then becoming that vision in our individual lives. What I love about where we are at this point in our history is that all angles of the Universe seem to point to the fact that who we are choosing to be matters, as it influences the world around us. Ancient wisdom, derived from spiritual texts, tells us this. Even science, through the study of things like mindfulness and quantum physics, details the universal connectedness of all things.

As I've observed our response to a hurting world, I've seen so many good people who want to truly make a difference, naively block the good that they wish to champion due to their lack of awareness of how the Universe works. Particularly as we've recently battled so many issues on so many fronts, we are essentially running around in circles, expending lots of energy but making very little progress. This is because we are using the tactics of an egoic mind to heal problems of the soul. Throughout the year, there's been a quote by activist Audre Lorde that keeps landing in my mind... "The master's tools will never dismantle the master's house."

Though Lorde was sharing her belief that the best way to change the world is by finding strength in our differences, for me, her words have also become a spiritual metaphor. We can't change the world by using the same tactics that created our challenges. This is akin to what Einstein meant when he said, "No problem can be solved from the same level of consciousness that created it." To shift towards a new world, rooted in love, we must use the tools of love to create it. This means that there must be a complete reframing of how we approach social justice and activism. For my part, I've outlined what I see as the fundamental shifts that must take place if we wish to truly make a difference and stand as powerful changemakers.

Don't Fixate on the Problem

I recently participated in a conference called "Hope Global Forums," which is spearheaded by entrepreneur and businessman John Hope Bryant. Each year, he convenes some of the best minds from across the country to discuss the problems that face underserved communities. This year, in a conversation with evangelist T.D. Jakes, Bryant talked about how our unrelenting focus on the problems that ail us is keeping us stuck and running in place. We are so fixated with what was and what is that there's no space to consider what "could be". In his own words, Bryant said, "Not only are we obsessed with the problem, but we're good at it." This way of constantly spotlighting problems poses a challenge because we grow things with our attention. Accordingly, we keep treading in the same cloudy waters. Instead, we must find a way to stop focusing on the pain and direct our energy towards the vision of what we want to create, holding onto it with such fierceness that we powerfully call it forth.

This is no different than how we must navigate our personal lives. If there's something you desire, be it a new car, a new house, or a new job, you will not attract it and bring it into manifestation by constantly focusing on all the things that are wrong with the one that currently belongs to you. Having panel discussions about the many challenges of the car that you currently own will only leave you depressed and in a low vibe space, rendering a path towards a new car inaccessible to you. You know how uncomfortable it is to ride in your current car. You know how unreliable it is on the road. There's no need to amplify these things over and over again.

The goal is to focus your attention on the vision of the new car that you desire, such that you feel its beauty and power. And when you're not visioning, you're maintaining your high vibration and creating the atmosphere for your new car (and all resonant good things) to find its way to you. Being in this space energizes you and feels good, thus delivering its own reward. But it also positions you to be able to clearly hear the guidance of your soul, which can easily detail a path to your new ride, in its own divine time.

Spiritual Teacher Esther Hicks, also known as Abraham Hicks, provides this example, "When you tune something with your radio dial... If you want to listen to a particular station, you've got to tune your tuner to the same frequency that what you are wanting to hear is being broadcast from. That's the way everything in the Universe is working. Your Source is broadcasting a signal, and you have the opportunity of tuning to that or not. When you tune to it, you feel wonderful. That's when you're at your clearest, or most fun, or most joyful, or your most vital. That's when you are energized. That's when you are full of you. You get what you think about whether you like it or not because when you're thinking about it, you're offering a signal."

As an African American, I carry a particular sensitivity to what I'm spotlighting. We have lived a legacy that's literally rooted in terror. And we've also lived a legacy that's rich with stories of how incredibly gifted, blessed, and wondrous we really are. Unfortunately, however, we spend an enormous amount of energy focusing on the terror of what was and the pain of its remnants that remain. While this is totally understandable, it leaves us more connected to a consciousness that is identified with victimhood than one that's identified with power. If we want to advance our cause, we must first embrace a knowing that we are divine creators capable of using the laws of the Universe to create the lives we desire. From there, we must learn to only tangentially point to the wrongs that must be made right and THEN, only as a small footnote on an elaborate PowerPoint presentation that's filled with love, light, and the vision of what we desire.

And just as it was illuminated in the example of our car, when we align with who we truly are, thereby reclaiming our inherent power, and dwell in high vibe spaces, then we can tune to the guidance of the Universe as it details a path to our lived desire.

Relatedly, we must be keenly aware of the damage we do to our kids when we, in our noble desire to protect them, lay the weight of the legacy of terror at their feet. Our children's minds are ripe with a readiness to absorb all things, and as they move through the world, they will bump into the programming that we have collectively forced upon them. If we condition them to believe that they have to work twice as hard to get ahead or that their blackness is something that could lead to their demise, they will project this into their lived reality. Or they will land as adults who must unlearn what they've been told, to be free. By handing down these stories, we unwittingly contribute to generational bondage.

I look forward to the day when "The Talk" has nothing to do with painting a picture of a dark past that still lurks in alleyways but, instead, includes the telling of the ancestral strength that runs through their veins and their own innate divine power. Let's teach them how to use their minds and hearts to positively shape their lives and this world. Let's tell them. Then they'll know. They do not have to buy into a narrative that they need anyone's approval before they can be free. The Universe itself is on their side. And as more and more of us believe this, this will become our collective reality.

Okay, I know you feel it. Yes, this conversation is something that has been on my heart for a while now. My people are too brilliant and wonderful to believe that we are at the mercy of needing anyone to "finally" render us free. Yes, racism is real, and our systems are riddled with inequality and disparities. Let's lead the charge in cleaning them up. But let's do it by leveraging the laws of the Universe. And let's do it knowing that as divine creators and children of God, our heaven on earth can be called forth now, through the power of our own minds. Peace, love, joy now... *while* doing the work of building systems that truly work for everyone.

This, of course, is the path for every person that belongs to a group that has been subjugated, not just blacks, because the same universal truths apply to us all. And for those who are a part of what we have labeled as privileged groups, whether that be whites, males, cisgender, heterosexual, etc., this labor of love is for you too. For your part, know that guilt and shame, because of the space that you occupy, are not warranted nor needed. This only further toxifies the world. However, if engaging in social justice reform and activism is a part of the work you've been called to do, know that, again, the same rules apply. Be aware of the problems, but don't fixate on them. Create and stand in your own vision of what an equal and just society looks like and align with your soul to be guided towards steps that will lead us all towards new land. Stay in your aligned, high vibe space as much as possible, knowing that you are painting the new world with your vibrations too. The prescription is the same... peace, love, joy... using it to contour a better world.

Use Your Anger Wisely

There's a lot of conversation about the role of anger in activism. As we previously discussed, depending on where you are on the emotional scale, anger can be a welcomed reprieve from lower-level vibrations such as grief or despair. It can be the thing that lights a fire and moves you towards hope. But the key is understanding that anger is still shy of empowerment. It's not a place where we want to take up residence for too long. You can and will make a greater difference if you release the anger and reach for authentic power. In the words of writer and freedom activist Jaiya John, "Your boundary need not be an angry electric fence that shocks those who touch it. It can be a consistent light around you that announces... I will be treated sacredly."

Also, the higher you move up on the vibrational scale, the higher your perspective and view of the terrain below. When you are in anger, your rage keeps you from seeing possibilities and resources that are available to you. Remember, when you are peaceful and calm, like still water, your perceptions are clear. You don't have access to this when you are stuck in anger. Use the anger, if it arises, to motivate you towards action. But once you become aware of it, shift to a higher vibration so your actions are fueled from an inspired and enlightened place.

Release the Fight Mentality

Another fundamental shift that's required is the need to shift from the "fight" mentality. As I mentioned before, force creates counterforce, and "what we resist persists." A push against anything will only strengthen it. This is true in our relationships, and it's true regarding activism. When we move forward in alignment with our divine nature, we are aligned with power itself. Force is not needed. We don't need to fight anything. We simply stand for that which we know to be true. No one describes this more masterfully than David Hawkins in his book, "Power vs. Force." Hawkins explains, "Force always moves against something, whereas power doesn't move against anything at all. Force is incomplete and therefore has to be fed energy constantly. Power is total and complete in itself and requires nothing from the outside. It makes no demands; it has no needs. Because force has an insatiable appetite, it constantly consumes. Power, in contrast, energizes, gives forth, supplies, and supports. Power gives life and energy – force takes these away."

If you are a part of a movement that feels weighted and exhausting, think about whether or not you are operating in your power or by force. When we awaken to our true power, en masse, allowing the strength of love to lead the way, the change that we want to see will arrive. Martin Luther King, Jr. said it best, "Power at its best is love implementing the demands of justice, and justice at its best is power correcting everything that stands against love."

Recognize that Your Level of Consciousness is Everything

The things that we create are infused with the energy that created them. This means everything that you do is influenced by your state of being when you do it. This is why it's so important to act from a place of alignment and to be clear on our intentions. If you do something with a spirit of peace and gentleness, then the thing you touch is marked by that essence. Conversely, if you do something with a spirit of angst, annoyance, resentment, or any other negative emotion, then the thing you touch is marked by *that* essence. The outcome will also be influenced accordingly. Remember, love moves by its own innate power and might.

Have you ever experienced something someone made for you, and you could feel that it was made with love? Our state of being is a force. It's unseen, but it's felt. And it's a force that infuses what we touch. So, if you are an activist, before you engage in the work, whether that's writing letters to decision-makers or joining in a march, check your intentions and infuse your efforts with love.

Love Power Tools

Appreciation

"Appreciation is the highest form of prayer,
for it acknowledges the presence of good wherever
you shine the light of your thankful thoughts."
– ALAN COHEN

Nothing has changed my life more dramatically than "Appreciation." It stands to reason that if "what we focus on expands," then when we find things to appreciate in our lives, those things will expand in our experience. If you want more of something, place your attention on it and show intense gratitude for it. And as you do, it will grow. Appreciation is intentional. It's walking through the world with a focused resolve to honor the beauty in everything. Appreciation and gratitude are often used interchangeably, but they are slightly different. Appreciation is an active, deliberate approach, whereas gratitude is more reflective. Gratitude, by definition, is "The quality of being thankful or grateful." Appreciation, by contrast, is defined as "A sensitive understanding of the aesthetic value of something". It is "love directed" or a focused love. To apply this tool in your life, you must look for goodness and beauty in the situations you face and the people with whom you interact.

Fear vs. Love

"It's true that there are only two primary emotions, love and fear. But it's more accurate to say that there is only love or fear, for we cannot feel these two emotions together, at exactly the same time. They're opposites. If we're in fear, we are not in a place of love. When we're in a place of love, we cannot be in a place of fear."
– ELISABETH KUBLER-ROSS

There are only two primal forces, fear and love. All negative emotions stem from fear, and positive emotions stem from love. You can determine what's fueling your actions based on how you feel in the moment. Negative... fear. Positive... love. Fear feels closed, constricted, and reactive, while love feels open, expansive, and proactive. Fear forces. Love allows. Fear feels like anger, shame, grief, guilt, judgment, blame, frustration, doubt, insecurity, hopelessness, etc. Love feels like joy, hope, peace, trust, confidence, connection, passion, freedom, harmony, honesty, acceptance, understanding, forgiveness, gratitude, compassion, etc. When you're moving through a situation, especially a challenging one, you can check in by feeling into your body to see if you're leaning towards fear or love. If you're feeling a negative emotion, first recognize it as fear and feel it fully, bringing an objective awareness to it. And when you're ready, take a deep breath, aim for a thought or affirmation that helps you to shift your perspective, and then consciously lean towards love. This tool can also be used in decision making by tuning in in the same way to determine what's fueling your choices.

Ho'oponopono

"You cannot love if you cannot forgive."
– KEMI SOGUNLE

Ho'oponopono is a Hawaiian practice of reconciliation and forgiveness, which means, "To make right." I am fascinated by it and find it very powerful. I use it to heal discord within myself and with others. Place your attention on the situation that's troubling you, whether that's another person, a group of people, or something within yourself, and recite the four steps over and over – or carry them with you throughout the day as a way to align with love. The beauty with this tool is it doesn't matter who's at fault or what went wrong. It opens and heals.

These are the four steps:

1. *I'm sorry.*
2. *Please forgive me.*
3. *Thank you.*
4. *I love you.*

Raise the vibe.

Love Reflective Questions

1. *What is life asking of you at this time?*

2. *To what degree have you consciously shaped your own life?*

3. *What could you do on a daily basis as an expression of love towards yourself?*

4. *If you were ready to truly allow your soul to take the lead in your life, what would be the hardest thing for you to surrender?*

5. *If you could receive any message from your soul, what are the words you most need to hear?*

6. *What do you need to say "Yes" to? What do you need to say "No" to?*

7. *Where, in your life, could you extend more grace to yourself? Others?*

Love Soul Quality

Grace

*"Alignment accounts for a lot, in making the journey that's yours
to make. Alignment is the direct path, the parallel gaze, the arrow
to its mark, the line of least resistance. Pick your metaphor... Grace,
though, Grace is the rain that moistens the soil of habit, the soil of
circumstance, and makes everything green and lush and beautiful.
Grass, flowers, bushes, trees, weeds, pavement, vacant lots...rain doesn't
discriminate, and neither does Grace. Grace makes herself available
to all. Grace offers herself without ever imposing. Grace."*
– HIRO BOGA

Grace... generosity and goodwill towards others.
Grace... acceptance and allowance.
Grace... forgiveness and surrender.
Grace... ease and effortlessness.
Grace... authentic beauty and charm.
Grace... unapologetic decency and goodness.
Grace... unmerited favor and love.

When we make our way to Love, we unlock grace. The most beautiful
soul quality of them all.

Coming Out Of The Closet

*"The most adventurous journey to embark on; is the journey
to yourself, the most exciting thing to discover; is who you
really are, the most treasured pieces that you can find;
are all the pieces of you, the most special portrait you can
recognize; is the portrait of your soul."*
– C. JoyBell C.

In 2011, I was listening to one of Dr. Sue Morter's audio recordings in preparation for my telesummit interview with her when something that she said astounded me. As she explained about our inherent power as divine beings, she said, "We are also the face of God." While it's quite possible that I'd heard these words before, from her or someone else, this felt like the first time I was truly *hearing* them. And in that moment, I took in the gravity of what that meant. As I interpreted it, Dr. Sue, in front of everyone, was declaring that we are not separate from that thing we call God... we are that! Though now, it feels like a "Yeah, duh" kind of statement, back then, I was seriously shaken. So much so that I went into my bedroom closet and called my sister-in-law because I needed to process. Because it landed with full resonance, the truthfulness of the statement was not in question, but I didn't know how to fully hold what she had shared.

Nearly panicked, I told my sister-in-law how this statement had landed on me and explained my concerns. What if Dr. Sue says something like this during my interview with her? And worse. What if someone in my family hears this? What will they think? Again, at that point, the idea felt almost subversive. And though my views about religion and spirituality were shifting and shifting fast, I had not fully disclosed my evolving beliefs to my tribe, who held beliefs that were different than my own. In addition to shifting towards the idea that there are many paths to that which we call God, I was now teetering even further over the line by declaring that God is us and we are God. True to form, my sister-in-law, in her calm wisdom, helped me to regain my sense of balance and breathe. I went on to conduct a lovely interview with Dr. Sue, and the sky did not fall.

Nevertheless, I often think about my "in the closet experience" because that was just the first coming out moment. Eventually, I made a decision that all of me was coming out. I felt no need to make declarations to anyone about anything, but I was no longer going to hide my beliefs or anything else. It was time to unleash THE most authentic version of Monica Moody.

I realized that I'd been muted in many ways. My personality, i.e., my commitment to be the grandest version of the real me, was not on full blast, and I wanted to change that. I wanted to be my enthusiastic, silly, uncensored, fun-loving, this-is-who-I-am, this-is-what-I-believe, and this-is-what-I'm-living-for, kind of self, no matter where I was, who I was with, and what I was doing. I wanted the True Me to take her rightful place in all areas of my life. It was time for her to be free.

Since then, I've continued to come out of the closet because once we start coming, the more we deepen within ourselves and the more there is to reveal. And I wouldn't have it any other way. This journey of aligning with our true divine nature is the work that we came here to do. It's the point of it all. And so, I hope that my words inspire you to come out of the closet as well. It's time for the True You to be free. If you use the shared tools and continue to return to the model, I assure you that a great work will unfold in you. But know that the invitation to awaken, align, flow, and love is not a model that you will move through one time, and then you're done. It's a model that you will cycle through over and over again as the True You takes flight. Best wishes to you, my friend. Shine on.

Now that you have read *Be Yourself to Free Yourself: Awakening to the Life You Are Meant to Live*, you are on your way towards aligning with your soul and reclaiming your authentic power! Plus, you are also equipped with tools and strategies that will aid you in moving towards your goals and dreams, with greater ease and grace.

As a thank you for purchasing my book, I've created several special bonuses to support you on your continued journey, including, (1) the **True You Personal Branding Playbook**, to assist you with bringing your personal and professional presence in alignment with the True You, (2) the **True You Meditation**, for sustained inspiration and renewal and (3) the **Be Yourself to Free Yourself Facilitator's Guide** for book clubs, so you can experience the book in community, for even greater accountability and impact, should you desire.

You can claim all of the bonus gifts here:

https://www.owningchange.com/true-you-bonus-gifts. And as another bonus, you'll receive periodic tips, tools and inspiration as a part of the Owning Change Community.

You are well-positioned to truly allow your soul to take the lead, as you move towards the liberated life you are meant to live. I'm in your corner and absolutely cheering you on.

Let me know if I can assist you in any way. Here's to powerfully living as the True You!

About the Author

Monica Moody is a guide and mentor for those who desire to recover and reclaim their authentic power, live purposefully, and move through their lives, towards their goals and dreams, with greater ease and grace.

A Certified Life Purpose and Career Coach, Spiritual Writer, Trainer and Facilitator, Monica shares practical, spiritual wisdom and details a path towards self-liberation and personal mastery. She believes that, by learning to embody the essential soul qualities of self-awareness, authenticity, vulnerability, responsibility, compassion, resilience, humility, and grace, we can each reclaim our personal power and create a brave new world.

Monica lives near Atlanta, Georgia with her husband and daughters and the rest of her huge family tribe.

Learn more at www.owningchange.com.